How Girls Can Help Their Country

Adapted from

Agnes Baden-Powell

and

Sir Robert Baden-Powell's

Handbook

1917

Contents

Part I.

Part II.

Part III.

Part IV.

Part V.

Part VI.

Copies of this book may be obtained from Girl Scout National Headquarters, 527 Fifth Avenue, City of New York; price 30 cents, postpaid.

PATRONESSES OF GIRL SCOUTS.

Mrs. Philip Brown .	. . . . .	New York
" Arthur Choate .	. . . .	" "
" Powers Farr .	. . . .	" "
" Snowdon Marshall	. . . .	" "
" Henry Parish, Jr. .	. . . .	" "
" Theodore Price	. . . .	" "
" Douglas Robinson .	. . . .	" "
" Samuel Van Dusen	. . . .	" "
" Leonard Wood .	. . . .	" "
" Wm. J. Boardman .	. . . .	Washington, D. C.
" Albert Burleson .	. . . .	" " "
" Jas. Marion Johnston	. . . .	" " "
" Joseph R. Lamar .	. . . .	" " "
" Richard G. Lay .	. . . .	" " "
" Oscar Underwood .	. . . .	" " "
" John Van Rensselaer .	. . . .	" " "
" Edward Douglas White	. . . .	" " "
" H. C. Greene .	. . . .	Boston, Mass.
Miss Katherine Loring .	. . . .	" "
" Louisa Loring .	. . . .	" "
Mrs. Ronald Lyman .	. . . .	" "
" Henry Parkman .	. . . .	" "
" William Lowell Putnam	. . . .	" "
" Lawrence Rotch .	. . . .	" "
" William W. Vaughan .	. . . .	" "
" Barrett Wendell .	. . . .	" "
" Roger Wolcott .	. . . .	" "
" William Ruffin Cox .	. . . .	Richmond Va.
" Hunter McGuire .	. . . .	" "
" Geo. Hyde Clark .	. . . .	Cooperstown, N. Y.
" Herbert Barry .	. . . .	Orange, N. J.
" Thomas Edison .	. . . .	" " "
" Philip McK. Garrison .	. . . .	" " "
" George Merck .	. . . .	" " "
" B. Palmer Axson .	. . . .	Savannah, Ga.
" George J. Baldwin .	. . . .	" "
Miss Elizabeth Beckwith .	. . . .	" "
Mrs. Rockwell S. Brank .	. . . .	" "
" W. W. Gordon .	. . . .	" "
" Louis W. Haskell .	. . . .	" "
Miss Hortense Orcutt .	. . . .	" "
" Nina Pape .	. . . . .	" "

Mrs. Frederick F. Reese. . . . Savannah, Ga.
" Samuel Drury . .St. Paul's School, Concord, N. H.
" Orton Brown . . . . . Berlin, N. H.
" Frederick Frelinghuysen . . . Newark, N. J.
" Wayne Parker . . . . " " "
" Douglas Gorman . . . . Baltimore, Md.
Miss Manly . . . . . " "
Mrs. Jas. Houstoun Johnston . . Birmingham, Ala.
" William S. Lovell . . . . " "
" Robert C. Alston . . . " "
" John B. Gordon . . . . Atlanta, Ga.
" Cleland Kinloch Nelson . . . " "
" John M. Slaton . . . . " "
" Carter Harrison . . . . Chicago, Ill.
" Herbert Havemeyer . . . " "
" Cyrus McCormick, Senior . . " "
Miss Skinner . . . . . " "
" Frederica Skinner . . . . " "
Mrs. Mark Willing . . . . " "
" Charles G. Washburn . . . Worcester, Mass.
Miss Katherine Hutchinson . . . Philadelphia, Pa.
Mrs. Robert Leslie . . . . " "
" John Markoe . . . . " "
" Alfonso Munoz . . . . " "
Miss Anne Thompson . . . . " "
Mrs. Charles Dobney . . . . Cincinnati, Ohio
" James Perkins. . . . . " "
Miss Josephine Simrall . . . . " "
Mrs. Robert Taft, Junior . . . " "
" Max Hirsch . . . . . " "
" G. S. Rafter . . . . . Washington, D. C.

Part I

HISTORY OF GIRL SCOUTS

GIRL Scouts, like Boy Scouts, are found all over the world. When Sir Robert Baden-Powell formed the first troops of Boy Scouts, six thousand girls enrolled themselves, but, as Sir Robert's project did not include the admission of girls, he asked his sister, Miss Baden-Powell, to found a similar organization for girls, based on the Boy Scout laws, with activities and occupations properly adapted for girls. She then founded the Girl Guide organization.

In America, in March, 1912, the first patrols of Girl Guides were enrolled by Juliette Low, in Savannah, Georgia. In 1913, the National Headquarters were established by her in Washington, D. C., and Miss Edith Johnston became the National Secretary. The name Girl Guides was then changed to Girl Scouts because the object of the organization is to promote the ten Scout Laws: TRUTH, LOYALTY, HELPFULNESS, FRIENDLINESS, COURTESY, KINDNESS, OBEDIENCE, CHEERFULNESS, PURITY, and THRIFT.

The movement then grew and spread in a remarkable way. The success of the movement is due, in a great measure, to the work of the National Secretary, Miss Cora Neal, who built up the organization during the most difficult years of its existence. In 1916, Headquarters were removed from Washington to New York, and the machinery for unifying the national work of the organization is now placed on an efficient basis.

The training of Girl Scouts is set forth in the Handbook, written by Lieut.-General Sir Robert Baden-Powell and Miss Baden-Powell.

Juliette Low obtained the rights of their book and, with the help of committees and experts from all parts of America, adapted it to the use of the Girl Scouts of the United States. It is impossible to train Girl Scouts without the Handbook.

In 1915, a Convention of Girl Scout leaders from most of the large cities was held and a National Council was formed, composed of delegates from the cities or communities where more than one hundred Girl Scouts were enrolled.

This National Council met in Washington, D. C., on June 10, 1915, and put the management of the business of the National Organization in the hands of an Executive Committee, composed of:

A President.
A Secretary or Executive Officer.
A Treasurer.
A Vice-President.
Chief Commissioner.
Six or more members of the National Council.

The Duties of the Executive Committee are:

(1) To grant charters to the Local Councils of Girl Scouts.

(2) To manufacture and copyright the badges.

(3) To select uniforms and other equipment.

At every annual meeting of the National Council there is an election of the Executive Committee. This committee has the power to cancel a charter.

National Headquarters

The National Headquarters has a staff of officers to do the work of the organization, holding their positions at the pleasure of the Executive Board. The National Secretary is appointed by the President and holds office at the pleasure of the President.

Each city or locality has a Local Council of twelve or more members, according to the size of the community. These local Councils are under the direction of the National Council and obtain their charters from Headquarters. Where one hundred or more Girl Scouts have been enrolled, the Local Council has the right to send one representative to the National Council for the annual meeting.

The salute is three fingers raised, the little finger held down by the thumb.

Handshake with the left hand while the right hand is raised in half salute—that is three fingers raised and held on the line with the shoulder. This is the salute given between one Girl Scout and another, and the full salute is when the fingers are raised to the temple on a level with the brow. This is given to officers and to the United States flag. (In saluting, the hand is always held upright, never in a horizontal position.)

The Salute

HOW TO BEGIN

It is not intended that Girl Scouts should necessarily form a new club separated from all others. Girls who belong to any kind of existing organization, such as school clubs or Y. W. C. A.'s may also undertake, in addition to their other work or play, the Girl Scouts' training and games, especially on Saturdays and Sundays.

It is not meant that girls should play or work on Sunday, but that they may take walks where they can carry on a study of plants and animals.

Groups or bands of girls not already belonging to any club may be organized directly as a Girl Scout Patrol or Troop.

How to Start a Patrol

Eight girls in any town, school, or settlement may join together to form a Patrol. They should have a Captain who must be at least twenty-one years old. The Captain selects a Lieutenant, or second in command, and the girls elect a Patrol leader. The girls should be from ten to seventeen years of age. It is best if all the girls in each Patrol are about the same age. A less number than eight girls can begin the movement, but eight girls are required to form a Patrol. A girl may not become a Lieutenant until she has reached the age of eighteen, or a Captain until she is twenty-one. In Europe, Girl Scout Patrols are sometimes formed by grown women who wish to carry out the Girl Scout program of preparedness. Members of such Patrols are called Senior Scouts. Senior Scouts make the three promises and accept the Scout law. They are enrolled as Scouts but do not meet regularly in the same manner as girls' Troops. They are organized in classes to learn first aid, signalling, marksmanship, or any other subject of

4

the Girl Scout program of training. Senior Scouts may well practice what they learn in such classes by teaching, for one or two months, Patrols of younger Girl Scouts. Thus they improve their command of what they have learned, and serve as an example to the younger Scouts, stimulating their interest in being prepared and especially in the subject taught.

The First Meeting

At the first meeting, the Scout Captain, who has previously studied the plan, principles, and object of the Girl Scout organization, explains the laws, promises, and obligations of the Girl Scouts to the members who are to form the troops. The names and addresses of the girls are recorded, the day set for the regular meeting, and the length of time for each meeting determined. Fifteen minutes may be spent on knot-tying, the Scout Captain first explaining the parts of the knot, and the requirements for knot-tying. Three-quarters of an hour to an hour should be spent on recreation out of doors.

Succeeding Meetings

The second, third, and fourth meetings should be spent in learning the requirements for the Tenderfoot tests. Each meeting should open with the formation of the troop in rank, by patrols, facing the Scout Captain. The first salute should be given to the Scout Captain, followed by the pledge to the flag, and inspection of the troop by the captain. After inspection the troop should break ranks and hold a short business meeting. Elections may be held at the second or third meeting for the patrol leader, corporal, secretary, treasurer, and any other officers the members of the troop may desire. The Scout Captain should instruct the troop how to conduct a business meeting, and explain the nomination and

election of officers. Weekly dues may be determined, **and** some decision had on the disposition of the funds. After the business meeting, the work or the tests should **be** studied, and the proper time spent on recreation. Every meeting should have a formal closing as well as a regular opening. For the closing, the troop should line up as for the opening routine, and give the good-bye salute. A definite time should be decided upon for the examination for Tenderfoot Scout, and the examination held at that time. Every Girl Scout who passes her examination is then ready to be enrolled and to make the Girl Scout Promise.

Girl Scout's Promise

Each girl must promise on her honor to try to do **three** things:

1. **To do my duty to God and to my country.**
2. **To help other people at all times.**
3. **To obey the laws of the Scouts.**

She learns the salute and the secret sign of the Scouts.

The Girl Scout Motto Is

These laws are for the guidance of Captains, and the girls, although they learn the Law, are not allowed to make the promise to keep the Law until the Captain considers · they are capable of living up to its spirit.

THE GIRL SCOUT LAWS

1.   A Girl Scout's Honor Is to be Trusted

If a Scout says, "on my honor it is so," that means that what she says is as true as if she had taken a most solemn oath.

2.   A Girl Scout Is Loyal

to the President, to her country, and to her officers; to her father, to her mother, and to her employers. She remains true to them through thick and thin.   In the face of the greatest difficulties and calamities her loyalty must remain untarnished.

3.   A Girl Scout's Duty Is to be Useful and to Help Others

She is to do her duty before anything else even if she gives up her own pleasure, safety, or comfort. When in doubt as to which of two things to do she must think, "Which is my duty?" which means, "Which is the best for other people?" and do that at once. She must be prepared at any time to save life or help the injured. She should do at least one good turn to someone every day.

4. **A Girl Scout Is a Friend to All, and a Sister to Every Other Girl Scout.**

Thus if a Scout meets another Scout, even though a stranger to her, she may speak to her, and help her in any way she can, either to carry out the duty·she is then doing or by giving her food, or as far as possible anything she may want. Like Kim a Scout should be a "Little friend to all the world."

5. A Girl Scout Is Courteous

That is, she is polite to all. She must not take any reward for being helpful or courteous.

6. A Girl Scout Keeps Herself Pure

in thought, word, and deed.

7. A Girl Scout Is a Friend to Animals

She should save them as far as possible from pain and should not kill even the smallest unnecessarily. They are all God's creatures.

8. A Girl Scout Obeys Orders

Under all circumstances, when she gets an order she must obey it cheerfully and readily, not in a slow, sullen manner. Scouts never grumble, whine, or frown.

9. A Girl Scout Is Cheerful

under all circumstances.

Scouts never grumble at hardships, nor whine at each other, nor frown when put out.

A Scout goes about with a smile and singing. It cheers her and cheers other people, especially in time of danger.

10. A Girl Scout Is Thrifty

This means, that a Scout avoids all useless waste of every kind; she is careful about saving every penny she can put into the bank so that she may have a surplus in time of need. She sees that food is not wasted, and that her clothing is cared for properly. The Girl Scout does not waste time. She realizes that time is the most precious thing any one of us has. The Girl Scout's time is spent either in useful occupations or in wholesome recreation, and she tries to balance these two harmoniously.

SELF-IMPROVEMENT
A Great Law of Life

One of the most fundamental laws of life is that, in the natural course of things, the influence of women over men is vastly greater than that of men over one another.

This is what gives to girls and women a peculiar power and responsibility, for no Girl Scout or other honorable woman—whether old or young—could use her influence as a woman excepting to strengthen the characters and to support the honor of the men and boys with whom she comes in contact.

Kipling, in Kim, says that there are two kinds of women,—one kind that builds men up, and the other that pulls men down; and there is no doubt as to where a Girl Scout should stand.

This great law is nothing to make a girl feel proud or superior to men; but, on the contrary, the understanding of it should make her humble and watchful to be faithful to her trust. Many a boy has been strengthened in his character and his whole life made happier by the brave refusal of a girl to do wrong; while the opposite weakness has been the cause of endless misery and wretchedness.

To gain and always retain the power to be a true woman friend to the men who belong in her own sphere of life is not always an easy matter for a girl, for she cannot do it unless she keeps a watch over her own faults and weaknesses so that the best of her is always in control. You can not fight for the right in the life of another unless you are first fighting for the right in your own life.

The chief difficulty in acquiring this happy and cheerful dignity comes from *the desire to be admired,* which is a tendency inborn in the great majority of women. It stands in the way of their greatest strength and usefulness, because it takes away their real independence and keeps them thinking about themselves instead of about others. It is a form of bondage which makes them vain and self-conscious and renders impossible the truest and happiest companionship between men and women friends.

"Be prepared," therefore, to do a true woman's full duty to her men by never allowing the desire for admiration to rule your actions, words, or thoughts. Our country needs women who are prepared.

Prepared for what?

To do their duty.

Be Strong

Have you ever stopped to think that your most constant companion throughout life will be yourself? You will always have this body, this mind, and this spirit that you call "I," but this body, this mind, this spirit are constantly growing and changing, and it is quite possible for the owner to direct this growth and

change. In order to live well, in order to possess the joy of life, and to be helpful to others, a Scout needs to apply her motto "Be prepared" to herself. Strength and beauty should be hers in body, mind, and spirit.

The body responds very readily to proper care and attention. In fact one may have the kind of body that she wishes, if a beginning is made in youth, and a plan persistently followed. The joyful exercise of vigorous outdoor games gives the finest type of training to the body, and at the same time the player enjoys the fun. To be happy and merry has a good effect itself on the body, while being angry or morose actually saturates the body with slow poisons. The body and mind are very closely related. Things that are good for one are good for the other. A girl who develops a strong agile body, at the same time improves her brain. A girl with weak, flabby muscles cannot have the strength of character that goes with normal physical power. It has been said, that "health is the vital principle of bliss, and exercise of health."

Be Helpful

To make others happy is the Scout's first wish. When you come home from work or school turn your thoughts to those you love at home and try to see what you can do to lighten their burdens or cheer them. It is not beyond the power of a girl to make home peaceful and happy. Perhaps there are little ones to think of. They are quick to copy and every good action and kind word of yours may have an effect on them through their whole lives.

DO A GOOD TURN to some one every day. That is one of the Scout laws. Tie a knot that you will have to untie every night, and before you go to sleep think of the good turn you did that day—if you find you have forgotten, or that the opportunity has not arisen that

day, do two next day to make up for it.   By your Scout's
oath you know you are in honor bound to try to do this.
It need be only a small thing.   Help some one across the
street or show him the way to the place he wishes to go.
Aid a person overburdened with packages, or pick one
up that has dropped.   Any little thing of this sort will
count.

Habits

"'Tis today we make tomorrow."   One of our wisest
men has said that each one of us is a bundle of habits.
We are so made that once we perform any act, that
particular thing is ever afterward easier to do.   We
tend to do the things we have already done.   By selecting the right things to do and always doing them, we
actually are making our destiny.   Each one of us has
her character made by her habits.   Habits are repeated
acts, and we may choose what our habits should be by
choosing our acts.   As Scouts we choose to be happy,
loyal, helpful girls.   As we practice the Scout laws they
become a part of us.

Modesty

Girl Scouts have often been complimented for their
modest bearing.   One does not hear them talk about
what they have done, or what they are going to do.
They just do the thing and say nothing about it.   They
go about their business or pleasure quietly and gently,
and never draw attention to themselves unnecessarily
by behaving noisily and talking or laughing loudly in
public.   They should be particularly careful of this
when in the company of boys or men.   Girls and boys
should be comrades and should never do anything to
lose the respect of older men and women.

Girls of good feeling should be especially careful to be

modest in dress and deportment on social occasions.
Unfortunately many girls who are perfectly innocent
and unconscious, cause comment and are the cause of
improper feelings being aroused among their companions.
Girls should not risk, by their manner of dress or method
of dancing, bringing temptation to others. It is easily
possible for a girl to exert an excellent influence upon her
friends by setting a proper example.

Reading

Wherever you go you will have the choice of good or
bad reading, and as reading has such a lasting effect on
the mind, you should try to read only good things. If
you find that you are tempted by reading rubbish, it is
easy to stop doing so. Once you know what your fault
is you can fight it squarely. Ruskin says, "All your
faults are gaining on you every hour that you do not
fight them."

The thing is, when there is danger before you, don't
stop and think about it,—the more you look at it the less
you will like it,—but take the plunge and go boldly in at
it, and it will not be half as bad as it looked, when you are
once in it. This is the way to deal with any difficulty in
life. If you have a job, or if any trouble arises which seems
too difficult to meet, don't shirk it—just smile, and try
and think out a way by which you may get successfully
through with it. Read in *Æsop's Fables* how the old
man advised his son that it was easy to break a bundle of
rods, but only if you took them one at a time.

Economy

More women are engaged in housekeeping than in all
the other professions and employments combined. This
is a difficult profession and requires knowledge and
training, if good results are to be secured. Housekeepers

need to have a plan, and especially a budget of expenses. One of the chief duties of housekeeping consists in seeing that there be no waste of any kind. The efficient house-keeper prevents a waste of food, of light, fuel, and of every other item. The wise individual gives special care to preventing a waste of time on the part of herself and others. The real orderly Girl Scout has a place for everything and keeps everything in its place. She has a time for performing each of her duties and does it at that time.

Thrift

It seems easy to learn how to spend money, but it is an art to learn how best to spend. Scouts gain experience by being allowed to purchase for the company, also by keeping the accounts, and they should always keep their own accounts neatly. We have to keep accounts when we grow up, and it is well to get into the way of measuring our expenditure from the first. You will remember that one of the Scout laws is to BE THRIFTY. The girl who begins making money young will go on making it as she grows older. It may be difficult at first, but it will come easier later on, especially if you earn money by hard work. If you try to make it only by easy means you are bound to lose after a time. Any number of poor girls have become rich, but in nearly every case it was because they meant to do so from the first. They worked for it and put every penny that could be spared into a savings account. The history of the majority of the world's greatest millionaires is that they began life without a dollar. To become a first-class Scout a girl must have a certain amount in the savings bank before she can have the honor of receiving her badge. By saving only two cents a week at least a dollar a year is saved.

Employment

"Stick to it" the thrush sings. One of the worst weaknesses of many people is that they do not have the perseverance to stick to what they have to do. They are always wanting to change. Whatever you take up, do it with all your might, and stick to it. Besides the professions of nursing, teaching, stenography and type-writing, and clerking, there are many less crowded employments, such as hair-dressing, making flowers, coloring photographs, assisting dentists, and gardening. There are many occupations for women, but before any new employment can be taken up one must begin while young to make plans and begin collecting information. "Luck is like a street car; the only way to get it is to look out for every chance and seize it—run at it and jump on; don't sit down and wait for it to pass. Opportunity is a street car which has few stopping places."

CHOOSE A CAREER: "Be prepared" for what is going to happen to you in the future. Try to master one trade so that you will be independent. Being punctual is a most important thing. This counts for a great deal in filling any kind of position.

Be Observant

In the early days of human development, centuries ago, the chief training men had was gained from fishing, hunting, and the other activities of savage life in the woods. This is a very valuable kind of training which city people miss. This knowledge of the woods, of animals and their habits, and of all the other phases of nature necessary for life in the open is called "Wood-craft." It is possible to train ourselves to be observant of nature and to develop a keenness of sight and hearing that are very valuable. It is a part of the duty of Scouts to see and appreciate the beauties of nature, and not be blind to them as so many people are.

Try to see everything. Consider it almost a disgrace if, when with others, they see anything big or small, high or low, near or far, that you fail to discover. See it first if you can.

Careers

Well educated women can make a good income by taking up translating, library work, architecture, and many professions which formerly have been open only to men. In Russia, a municipal fire brigade has been commanded by a young woman. The medical profession offers a great opportunity to women. Nursing is more easily learned, and is of the greatest advantage at the same time, for every woman is a better wife and mother for having been a nurse first. Even so long ago as the first century women devoted their lives to the medical profession, as Zenais, a relative of St. Paul, Leonilla, and Hildegarde of Mont Rupert. Later, Nicerate, in 404, studied medicine and practiced with great ability. Fifty years ago no woman could become a doctor. Now it is within the power of any intelligent girl, through study and perseverance, to enter the medical profession, and even to rise to distinction and to honorable celebrity, Mme. Curie has done such wonderful work in chemistry, that the Academy of Paris has long debated whether she should not be made an academician for her discoveries in connection with polonium and radium.

Study

Each one of us has her own destiny in her control, and has her own personal problems in life to settle. Thus, we all need all the knowledge and wisdom that we can secure. Each one of us should be a student, ever growing in power of thought and in usefulness to others. Too many people think that education consists in memorizing all kinds of information exactly as it is put down in the books. What each one of us really needs is to have a mind that can think definitely and intelligently upon all the problems presented in life. It is possible for us to train our minds for this kind of useful and independent thought. In the first place we should select subjects for study that are of real interest because they bear upon some problem that concerns us. Whenever we begin to read a book, or undertake any topic of study, it should be done with a definite purpose in mind. Propose to yourself some question that you expect to be answered by this book, or by this subject. Do not be satisfied with the statement of one author, but also find out what other authors say, and what some of your friends think upon this question. When you have done this, try to arrange the different thoughts and statements according to a plan. Pick out the largest truth in the whole matter and arrange other statements or thoughts as they are related to this central one. Making an outline of a book is an excellent plan. Do not commit yourself entirely to the author's point of view, if it does not agree with your own. Each one of us has a distinct individuality and is entitled to his own views, to a certain extent. However, we should keep our minds open, ready to accept new truths as they are brought to our attention. Science and knowledge are constantly advancing, and what we believe now, we may find, some years hence, to be only a part of the truth. Thus, it is not necessary to memorize lessons and subjects until after we have thought out what the real meaning is, and arranged the whole subject on a definite plan. Then, we will usually find that we know the topic without having to memorize it formally. Finally we should try to put to use the ideas we have gained. The real value of ideas lies in making them serve us. When you have actually put into practice some bit of knowledge, you may then feel that it really belongs to you.

In our work and study we need to learn to devote our whole attention to one thing,—to do this one thing with all the power that we have. Too many of us form a habit of dividing our attention, trying to carry two things in mind at the same time. This is a weakness that interferes with our success. If we are truly interested, we should put our whole attention upon the one matter and develop power of concentration.

To make what has been said about study clearer, let us use an illustration. Suppose one of our Girl Scouts is fond of gardening. The family has no garden, and there is a vacant space in the yard that could be used for this purpose. She begins the reading of one of the farmers' bulletins on this subject, and has in mind, all the time, making a garden of her own. This object of making her own garden is her guide in the study. She wishes to learn what plants are best suited to her plot, which ones will give her the best return for the kind of soil that she has, and so, as she reads, she chooses for herself from the ideas that are presented. The whole subject is arranged in her own mind around her own plan of making a garden. After reading this bulletin she is likely to consult her friends who know anything about this subject, and to read other articles. Finally she puts into practice the notions she has gathered, and finds through actual trial whether they succeed or not. If she is successful in growing flowers and vegetables, the ideas have been put to a very practical and beneficial use. This girl will know a great deal more about gardening than if she merely read the book.

Patriotism

You belong to the great United States of America, one of the great world powers for enlightenment and liberty. It did not just grow as circumstances chanced to form it. It is the work of your forefathers who spent brains and blood to complete it. Even when brothers fought they fought with the wrath of conviction, and when menaced by a foreign foe they swung into line shoulder to shoulder with no thought but for their country.

In all that you do think of your country first. We are all twigs in the same fagot, and every little girl goes to make up some part or parcel of our great whole nation.

Part II

MEMBERSHIP

This Organization is Non-Sectarian and Non-Political

ANY girl over ten years old may become a Girl Scout and she may belong to other organizations at the same time.

She first ranks as Tenderfoot or third-class Girl Scout, then, after one month, she becomes, after passing certain tests, a second-class Girl Scout, and finally attains the rank of first-class Girl Scout.

After she has reached the age of eighteen, a girl can become a lieutenant, and when she is twenty-one years old she may become a captain if she has passed the first-class examinations. Girl Scouts' patrols in Europe are sometimes formed by grown-up women, who wish to carry out the Girl Scout program of preparedness, and these are called Senior Scouts.

Grades

Tenderfoot
Second Class
First Class

Officers of the Local Organization

A Commissioner. The duties of a Commissioner are:

To inspect companies and patrols and advise how to conduct them according to the principles found in the Handbook.

To secure the harmonious co-operation of all the captains in the district.

To be the authority for recommending the issue or the denial of captains' certificates before they are sent to Headquarters.

To foster the movement generally throughout the district. (Where there is no Secretary, the Commissioner must organize the examinations for Merit Badges.)

To forward the semi-annual reports to Headquarters.

A Secretary. The duty of a Secretary is to be the local executive officer.

She shall have charge of Headquarters and other property of the local organization.

She shall have a general supervision of the captains and instruct new captains in their duties.

She shall keep a record of all the troops, the names and addresses of the captains and the councilors of Girl Scouts, and such other information in regard to them as may be necessary for her work. She shall receive all the applications for Girl Scout captains' certificates and send these applications to Headquarters. Where a local council exists, all applications must be approved by the local council.

She shall render a report at the regular meetings of the local board of councilors on the condition and progress of the Girl Scouts.

She shall notify all the members of the annual, regular, and special meetings.

She shall attend all the public meetings connected with the organization.

A Treasurer. The duties of a Treasurer:

She shall keep an itemized account of all receipts and disbursements in a book, and present a written report at the regular meeting of the board of councilors.

She shall pay only those bills that have been signed by the Commissioner and Secretary.

She shall make an annual report and produce the vouchers which shall be submitted to an auditor at least one week before the annual meeting.

All the local organization's funds shall pass through her hands.

A Captain.   The duties of a Captain:

The captain has the power to enroll Scouts and to recommend them to the local committee for badges and medals. She also has the power to release a Scout from her promise, and to withdraw her badges at any time, and to discharge her. A Scout who considers herself unjustly treated may appeal to the local council. Their decision shall be final.

The captain must apply to National Headquarters for an official certificate. Her application must be accompanied by the names of two prominent citizens, and in places where a local council is established her application must be sent through the local council or court of honor and be endorsed by one member of the council.

The qualifications for a captain shall be:

A general knowledge of the Handbook for Girl Scouts.

A full appreciation of the religious and moral aim underlying the practical instruction of the entire scheme of training.

Personal standing and character such as will insure a good moral influence over the girls, and sufficient steadfastness of purpose to carry out the work with energy and perseverance.

Age not less than twenty-one years.

A captain is assumed to have passed the first-class Scout Test. She wears the all-round cords, if she prefers to do so, instead of putting on all the separate badges as the girls do.

Captains may join the Red Cross or any other organization or club.

Officers' certificates must be returned if the officer resigns or if the certificate is cancelled, as these are the property of the President.

A Lieutenant:

The duties of a lieutenant are the same as those of a captain in the absence of the captain. She is chosen by the captain to work with her, and must be over eighteen years of age. Lieutenants may wear captains' badges after passing the first-class test.

A Patrol Leader is selected in each patrol by the girls themselves (or, if the girls desire it, by the captain). She holds her office for six months or a year. The girls are apt to select the right girl for the place.

The patrol leader must be what her name implies, "A Leader," for she stands next to the captain and lieutenant, and takes either place in their absence. The patrol must not look upon her as a "Boss." This feeling must not enter into the patrol affairs at all, but the girls must remember that they have put her there, and they must do all they can to uphold her and support her in the work. If she is the right sort of girl no such feeling will arise. If a patrol leader gives an order that a Girl Scout does not like or think fair, the Scout must obey the order, but later on she may talk it over with her patrol leader. If, still, she is dissatisfied, she may go to her captain, who must decide the matter. If the patrol leader is not a good officer, the captain may reduce her to Scout rank and have another election.

The patrol leader appoints one of her girls as a Corporal, who takes her place when she is absent, and assists her in keeping the patrol leader's books.

The duties of the patrol leader are to call the roll and keep a record of attendance of her patrol.

The patrol leader keeps a record of the dues. Patrol leaders' registers may be obtained at Headquarters.

The patrol leader is responsible for leaving the club

room in perfect order. She may have her corporal assist her in tidying up, or she may choose some girls to help her.

Patrol Officers:

Each patrol selects its own secretary or scribe.

The duties of a secretary: To keep a record of what is done at the meetings; to receive and answer letters.

Patrol Nurse. The duty of a patrol nurse is to take care of any accidents to the girls during a hike or a picnic. She should possess a first-aid kit.

QUALIFICATIONS FOR THE THREE GRADES OF GIRL SCOUTS

The Tests

A Tenderfoot (Badge, a Brooch) must be ten years old.

Before making the Scout Promise, she must know:

How to tie four of the following knots: reef, sheet-bend, clove hitch, bowline, fisherman's, and sheep-shank (see p. 68).

The name of the Governor of the State and of the Mayor of the city.

The History of the Flag, and how to fly it (see p. 135).

The ten Scout Laws.

A Second-Class Girl Scout (Badge, worn on left arm) must have had one month's service as Third-Class Scout. She must pass the following tests:

Must have made a drawing of, or cut out and made in cloth or on paper, the Flag of the United States.

Know how to cook one simple dish, such as potatoes or a quarter of a pound of meat.

Lay a fire in stove, or light a fire in the open with two matches.

Make a bed properly, and know how to make an invalid's bed.

Know her own measurements (see cards at Headquarters for details of measurement).

Must know the eight points of the compass (see compass, p. 71).

Must know what to do in case of fire (see p. 125).

Must know remedy for poison ivy and what to do to prevent frostbite (see pp. 134 and 135).

25

Must know health habits (page 96).

Must know how to work a buttonhole, or knit or crochet, sew a seam and hem a garment.

Must know Morse alphabet or semaphore alphabet.

A First-Class Scout (Badge, sewn on left sleeve above elbow, which entitles the wearer to go in for all-round cords) must have gained a Second-Class Badge.

Must know how to set a table properly for breakfast, dinner, and supper.

Bring a shirt-waist or skirt sewn by herself or equivalent needlework.

Be able to describe how to get a specified place and walk one mile in twenty minutes.

Must be able to dress and bathe a child two years old or younger (see p. 122).

Be able to pass an examination upon the first three chapters of the woman's edition of the American Red Cross Abridged Text-Book in First Aid.

Must have knowledge of signaling and of semaphore code or International alphabet (p. 75), writing 32 letters per minute.

Must have 50 cents in savings bank earned by herself.

Must produce a girl trained by herself in tests, Tenderfoot Class.

Know how to distinguish and name ten trees, ten wild flowers, ten wild animals, ten wild birds.

Must know simple laws of sanitation, health and ventilation (pp. 111 to 115).

Swim fifty yards in her clothes or show a list of twelve satisfactory good turns.

Show points of compass without a compass.

Must give correctly the Scouts' secret passwords.

The subjects for proficiency badges may be undertaken after a girl becomes a Second-Class Girl Scout, and the interest in her work is thus continuous. The badges for proficiency are registered and are issued only by Headquarters.

ENROLLMENT

Ceremony of Investiture of Scouts

THE ceremonial for a Tenderfoot to be invested as a Scout should be a serious and earnest function. The captain calls "Fall in." The patrol is formed in a horseshoe, with captain and lieutenant in the gap, and the American flag spread out. The Tenderfoot, with her patrol leader (who will already have taught her tests and knots), stands just inside the circle, opposite the captain. "Salute." All salute her. The lieutenant holds the staff and hat, shoulder-knot and badge, and neckerchief of the Tenderfoot. When ordered to come forward by the captain, the patrol leader brings the Tenderfoot to the center. The captain then asks: "Do you know what your honor means?"

The Tenderfoot replies: "Yes, it means that I can be trusted to be truthful and honest"—(or words to that effect).

Captain: "Can I trust you on your honor to be loyal to God and the country, to help other people at all times, and to obey the Scout Law?"

The Tenderfoot then makes the half salute, and so do the whole company, whilst she says: "I promise, on my honor to be loyal to God and my country, to help other people at all times, and to obey the Scout Law."

The captain then says: "I trust you, on your honor, to keep this promise."

Whilst the recruit is making her promises aloud, all the Scouts remember their own promises, and vow anew to keep them.

The captain orders: "Invest."

The patrol leader then steps out, gives the Tenderfoot her staff, and puts her hat, neckerchief, and knot on her.

27

She then marches up the line to the captain, who pins on her trefoil badge, and explains that it is her Scout's "life." If, for misbehavior, her trefoil or life has to be taken from her, she becomes a dead Scout for the time the captain orders—a day or a week—and is in disgrace. The badge may be worn at all times, but the uniform is worn only when the patrol meets.

The new Scout is then initiated into the mysteries of secret passwords Be Prepared (said backwards). The captain orders: "To your patrol—quick march."

The whole patrol salute and shoulder staves; the new Scout and her patrol leader march back to their places.

These badges being the registered designs of the Corps, do not belong to the girls who have passed the tests.

The equipment does not belong to the girl except by special permission.

Any person wearing Girl Scouts' badges without permission is liable to be prosecuted according to law, and may incur a penalty. Offenses, such as people who are not enrolled saluting, outsiders wearing Girl Scouts' badges, or "Monkey" patrols wearing Girl Scouts' uniforms, must be dealt with by trial at a Court of Honor to determine the forfeit or penalties to be imposed on the culprits.

Captains have the power to dismiss a Scout, and the badge and the buttons of her uniform must then be returned.

BADGES AND AWARDS

The Badge

The Girl Scout badge is a clover leaf, the three leaves representing the Girl Scout promises: (1) To do her duty to God and her country. (2) To help other people at all times. (3) To obey the Scout law.

When to Wear the Badge

A girl asked me what were the occasions on which she might wear her badge, thinking it was not for everyday use. The reply was, "You may wear your badge any day and any hour when you are doing what you think is right. It is only when you are doing wrong that you must take it off; as you would not then be keeping your Scout promises. Thus you should either take off the badge, or stop doing what you think is wrong."

The " Thanks " Badge

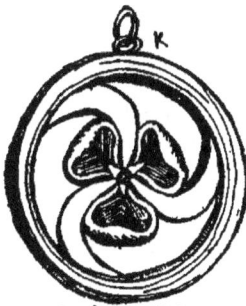

The "Thanks" badge may be given to any one to whom a Girl Scout owes gratitude. Every Girl Scout throughout the whole world when she sees the thanks badge, recognizes that the person who wears it is a friend and it is her duty to salute and ask if she can be of service to the wearer of the badge.

The "Thanks" Badge.

The approval of National Headquarters must be obtained before a thanks badge is presented to any one.

Medals for Meritorious Deeds

These medals are granted only by Headquarters, or by the President on special recommendation from the captain, who should send in a full account with written evidence from two witnesses of the case.

These are worn on the right breast, and are awarded as follows:

Life-Saving Medals

The Bronze Cross. (Red Ribbon.) Presented as the highest possible award for gallantry, this medal may be won only when the claimant has shown special heroism or has faced extraordinary risk of life in saving life.

The Silver Cross (Blue Ribbon) is given for gallantry, with considerable risk to herself.

The Badge of Merit (Gilt Wreath. White Ribbon), for a Scout who does her duty exceptionally well, though without grave risks to herself, or for specially good work in recruiting on behalf of the Girl Scout movement, or for especially good record at school for one year in attendance and lessons is awarded when full records of such deeds accompany the claim.

Bronze and Silver Cross for Saving Life.

Gilt Medal of Merit.

How to Become a "Golden Eaglet"

To secure this honor a Girl Scout must win fourteen of the following badges: Ambulance, Clerk, Cook,

Child-nurse, Dairy-maid, Matron, Musician, Needlewoman, Naturalist, Sick-nurse, Pathfinder, Pioneer,
Signaler, Swimmer, Athletics, Health or Civics.

In examining for tests one of the Court of Honor
should, if possible, be present.

The Local Committee should be satisfied, through the
recommendation of the girls' captain, that the tests were
satisfactorily performed.

TESTS FOR MERIT BADGES

A girl must become a Second Class Scout before she is
eligible for the proficiency tests. Merit badges are
issued to those who show proficiency in the various
subjects listed in this chapter. These badges are registered at Headquarters and are issued from no other
source.

The purpose of the various tests is to secure continuity
of work and interest on the part of the girls.

The girl who wins one of these merit badges has her
interest stimulated and gains a certain knowledge of the
subject. It is not to be understood that the knowledge
required to obtain a badge is sufficient to qualify one
to earn a living in that branch of industry.

Merit Badges

1. Ambulance. (Maltese Red Cross.)
To obtain a badge for First Aid
or Ambulance a Girl Scout must
have knowledge of the Sylvester or
Schaefer methods of resuscitation in
cases of drowning.

Must pass examination on first
three chapters of Woman's Edition
of Red Cross Abridged Text Book
on First Aid.

Treatment and bandaging the injured (p. 131).
How to stop bleeding (p. 133).
How to apply a tourniquet (p. 134).
Treatment of ivy poison (p. 134).
Treatment of snake-bite (p. 59).
Treatment of frost-bite (p. 135).
How to remove cinder from eye (p. 124).

2.   Artist.   (Palette.)

To obtain an artist's badge a Girl Scout must draw or paint in oils or water colors from nature; or model in clay or plasticine or modeling wax from plaster casts or from life; or describe the process of etching, half-tone engraving, color printing or lithographing; or

Arts and Crafts:
Carve in wood; work in metals; do cabinet work.

3.   Athletics.   (Indian Clubs.)
To obtain this badge a Scout must:
  1.   Write a 500-word article on value of Athletics to girls, giving proper method of dressing and naming activities most beneficial.
  2.   Be a member of a gymnasium class of supervised athletics or a member of an active team for field work.
  3.   Understand the rules of basket ball, volley ball, long ball, tether ball, tennis and captain ball.
  4.   Must be able to float, swim, dive and undress in water.
  5.   Know and be able to teach twenty popular games.

4. Attendance. (Annual.) (Badge, Silver Star.)
Must complete one year of regular attendance.

5. Automobiling. (A Wheel.)
   1. Must pass an examination equal to that required to obtain a permit or license to operate an automobile in her community.
   2. Know how to start a motor and be able to do it and be able to explain necessary precautions.
   3. Know how to extinguish burning oil or gasoline.
   4. Comply with such requirements as are imposed by body conducting the test for licensing drivers.

6. Aviation. (Monoplane.)

   To obtain a merit badge for aviation, a Scout must:
   1. Have a knowledge of the theory of the aeroplane, helicopter, and ornithopter, and of the spherical and dirigible balloon.
   2. Have made a working model of any type of heavier than air machine, that will fly at least twenty-five yards; and have built a box kite that will fly.
   3. Have a knowledge of the types and makes of engines used for aeroplanes, of the best known makes of aeroplanes, and of feats performed or of records made by famous aviators.
   4. Have a knowledge of names of famous airships (dirigibles) and some of their records.
   5. Understand the difference between aviation and aerostation, and know the types of apparatus which come under these two heads.

3

7. Bird Study. (Bird.)

To secure this badge a Scout must:
1. Give list of 30 well known wild birds of United States.
2. State game bird laws of her State.
3. Give list of 30 wild birds personally observed and identified in the open.
4. Give list of 10 wild birds sold as cage birds.
5. Name 10 birds that destroy rats and mice.
6. Give list of 25 birds of value to farmers and fruit growers in the destruction of insect pests on crops and trees.
7. Give name and location of 2 large bird refuges, explain the reason for their establishment and the birds they protect.
8. Tell what the Audubon Society is and how it endeavors to conserve the birds of beautiful plumage.
9. What an aigret is, how obtained, and from what bird. (*Land Birds and Water Birds*, C. A. Reed.) (The Department of Agriculture has a number of bulletins on birds. See list.)
10. What methods to attract birds winter and summer.

8. Boatswain. (Anchor.)

To obtain a badge for seamanship a Girl Scout must:
1. Be able to tie six knots.
2. Be able to row, pole, scull, or steer a boat.
3. Land a boat and make fast.
4. State directions by sun and stars.
5. Swim 50 yards with clothes and shoes on.
6. Box the compass and have a knowledge of tides.
7. Know rules of the road for steamers and power boats, also lights for boats underway. See Pilot Rules, Gov. Ptg. Office, Washington, D. C.

9. **Child-Nurse. (Green Cross.)**

To obtain this badge a Girl Scout must:

1. Take care of a child for two hours each day for a month, or care for a baby for one hour a day for a month.

2. Know how to bathe and dress a baby.

    (Examination should be made with infant present, if possible.)

3. Should understand care of children, have elementary knowledge as to their food, clothing, etc.

4. Know three kindergarten games and describe treatment of simple ailments.

5. Be able to make poultices, and do patching and darning.

6. Know how to test bath heat and use of thermometer; count the pulse (p. 123).

10. **Clerk. (Pen and Paper.)**

1. Must have legible handwriting; ability to typewrite; a knowledge of spelling and punctuation; a library hand; or, as an alternative, write in shorthand from dictation at twenty words a minute as a minimum.

2. Ability to write a letter from memory on a subject given verbally five minutes previously.

3. Knowledge of simple bookkeeping and arithmetic.

4. Keep complete account of personal receipts and expenditure for six months, or household accounts for three months.

11. Civics. (Eight-point Star.)

To obtain this badge a Scout must:

1. Be able to recite the preamble to the Constitution.
2. Be able to state the chief requirements of citizenship of a voter, in her state, territory or district.
3. Be able to outline the principal points in the naturalization laws in the United States.
4. Know how a president is elected and installed in office, also method of electing vice-president, senators, representatives, giving the term of office and salary of each.
5. Be able to name the officers of the President's Cabinet and their portfolios.
6. The number of Justices of the Supreme Court of the United States, the method of their appointment and the term of office.
7. Know how the Governor of her state, the lieutenant-governor, senators and representatives are elected and their term of office. Also explain the government of the District of Columbia and give the method of filling the offices.
8. Know the principal officers in her town or city and how elected and the term of office.
9. Know the various city departments, and their duties, such as fire, police, board of health, :harities and education.
10. Be able to name and give location of public buildings and points of interest in her city or town.
11. Tell the history and object of the Declaration of Independence.

12. Cook. (Gridiron.)

1. Must know how to wash up, wait on table, light a fire, lay a table for four, and hand dishes correctly at table.
2. Clean and dress fowl.
3. Clean a fish.
4. How to make a cook place in the open.
5. Make tea, coffee or cocoa, mix dough and make bread in oven and state approximately cost of each dish.
6. Know how to make up a dish out of what was left over from the meals of the day before.
7. Know the order in which a full course dinner is served.
8. Know how to cook two kinds of meat.
9. Boil or bake two kinds of vegetables successfully.
10. How to make two salads.
11. How to make a preserve of berries or fruit, or how to can them.
12. **Estimate cost of food per day for one week.**

13. Invalid Cooking. (A palm leaf.)

1. How to make gruel, barley water, milk toast, oyster or clam soup, beef tea, chicken jelly.

14. Cyclist. (A Wheel.)

1. Own a bicycle.
2. Be able to mend a tire.
3. Pledge herself to give the services of her bicycle to the government in case of need.
4. If she ceases to own a bicycle, she must return the badge.

5. Read a map properly.
6. Know how to make reports if sent out scouting on a road.

15. Dairy. (Sickle.)

1. Know how to test cow's milk with Babcock Test (p. 119).
2. To make butter.
3. How to milk.
4. Know how to do general dairy work, such as cleaning pans, etc., sterilizing utensils.
5. Know how to feed, kill, and dress poultry.
6. Test five cows for ten days each with Babcock Test and make proper reports.

16. Electricity. (Lightning.)

To obtain a merit badge for Electricity, a Scout must:

1. Illustrate the experiment by which the laws of electrical attraction and repulsion are shown.
2. Understand the difference between a direct and an alternating current, and show uses to which each is adapted. Give a method of determining which kind flows in a given circuit.
3. Make a simple electro-magnet.
4. Have an elementary knowledge of the construction of simple battery cells, and of the working of electric bells and telephones.
5. Be able to replace fuses and to properly splice, solder, and tape rubber-covered wires.
6. Demonstrate how to rescue a person in contact with a live electrical wire, and have a knowledge of the method of resuscitation of a person insensible from shock.

17. Farmer. (Sun.)

1. Incubating chickens, feeding and rearing chickens under hens.
2. Storing eggs (p. 116).
3. Knowledge of bees.
4. Swarming, hiving and use of artificial combs.
5. Care of pigs.
6. How to cure hams (p. 120).
7. Know how to pasteurize milk (page 116).

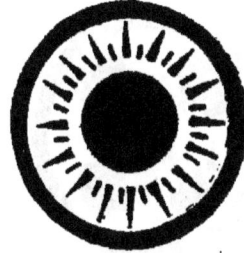

18. **Gardening.** (A Trowel.)

1. Participate in the home and school garden work of her community.
2. Plan, make and care for either a back-yard garden, or a window garden for one season.
3. Give plan of her work, the flowers or vegetables planted, the size and cost of her plot and the profit gained therefrom.
4. She must also supervise or directly care for the home lawns, flower beds; attend to the watering, the mowing of the grass, keeping yards free from waste paper and rubbish, to the clipping of shrubbery and hedges.

This test is open to scouts already in the Girls' Garden and Canning Clubs throughout the country and a duplicate of their reports, sent in for their season's work, to the state agricultural agents, or agricultural colleges, in co-operation with the Department of Agriculture of the United States, may be submitted as their test material for this badge.

Farmers' Bulletins, 218, 185, 195.

19. Personal Health.   (Dumb-bells.)

To obtain a badge for personal health, a Scout must:

1. Eat no sweets, candy, or cake between meals for three months.
2. Drink nothing but water, chocolate, or cocoa for a year.
3. Walk a mile daily for three months.
4. Sleep with open window.
5. Take a bath daily for a year, or sponge bath.
6. Write a statement of the care of the teeth, and show that her teeth are in good condition as a result of proper care.
7. Tell the difference in effect of a cold bath and a hot bath.
8. Describe the effect of lack of sleep and improper nourishment on the growing girl.
9. Tell how to care for the feet on a march.
10. Describe a good healthful game and state its merits.
11. Tell the dangers of specialization and over-training in the various forms of athletics, and the advantages of an all-around development.
12. Give five rules of health which if followed will keep a girl healthy **(page 96).**

20. Public Health.   (U. S. A. Flag.)

1. Write an article, not over 500 words, about the country-wide campaign against the housefly, and why, giving the diseases it transmits and make a diagram showing how the fly carries diseases, typhoid, tuberculosis and malaria. (See *Public Health Service Bulletins* on these subjects.)

(Also see page 117.)

2. Tell how to cleanse and purify a house after the presence of contagious disease.

3. State the laws of her community for reporting contagious disease.

4. Tell how a city should protect its supplies of milk, meat and exposed foods.

5. Tell how these articles should be cared for in the home. (See *Farmers' Bulletin*—" Care of Food in the Home.") (Also see pages 115 and 116.)

6. Tell how her community cares for its garbage.

7. State rules for keeping Girl Scout camp sanitary —disposal of garbage, rubbish, etc.

21. Horsemanship. (Spur.)

1. Demonstrate riding at a walk, trot and gallop.

2. Know how to saddle and bridle a horse correctly, and how to groom a horse properly.

3. Know how to harness correctly in a single or double harness, and how to drive.

4. Know how to tether and hobble and when to give feed and drink

5. State lighting up time, city law.

6. How to stop run-away horse (page 135).

22. Home-Nursing. (Red Cross, Green Ring.)

1. Must pass tests recommended by American Red Cross Text Book and Elementary Hygiene and Home Care of the Sick, by Jane A. Delaro, Department of the American Red Cross. These tests may be had from Headquarters, upon request.

2. Know how to make invalid's bed.

3. Know how to take temperature; how to count pulse and respirations.

4. Know how to prepare six dishes of food suitable to give an invalid.

23. Housekeeper. (Crossed Keys.)
    1. Tell how a house should be planned to give efficiency in housework.
    2. Know how to use a vacuum cleaner, how to stain and polish hardwood floors, how to clean wire window screens, how to put away furs and flannels, how to clean glass, kitchen utensils, brass and sinks.
    3. Marketing.
    Know three different cuts of meat and prices of each.
    Know season for chief fruits and vegetables, fish and game.
    Know how flour, sugar, rice, cereals and vegetables are sold; whether by packages, pound, or bulk, quarts, etc.
    4. Tell how to choose furniture.
    5. Make a list of table and kitchen utensils, dishes for dining-room and glasses necessary for a family of four people.
    6. How to make a fireless cooker, small refrigerator and window box for winter use.
    7. Prepare a budget showing proper per cent of income to be used for food, shelter, clothing, savings, etc.

24. Interpreter. (Clasped Hands.)
    1. Be able to carry on a simple conversation in any other language than her own.
    2. Write a letter in a foreign language.
    3. Read or translate a passage from a book or newspaper in French, German, Italian, or in any other language than her own.

25. Laundress. (Flatiron.)

1. Know how to wash and iron a garment, clear starch and how to do up a blouse.
2. Press a skirt and coat.
3. Know how to use soap and starch, how to soften hard water, and how to use a wringer or mangle.

26. Marksmanship. (Rifles.)

1. Pass tests in judging distances, 300 to 600 yards and in miniature rifle shooting, any position, twenty rounds at 15 or 25 yards, 80 out of 100.
2. Know how to load pistol, how to fire and aim or use it.
3. Or be proficient in fencing or archery.

27. Music. (Harp.)

1. Know how to play a musical instrument. Be able to do sight reading. Have a knowledge of note signs and terms.
2. Name two master composers and two of their greatest works.
3. Be able to name all of the 25 instruments in the orchestra in their proper order.
4. Never play rag time music, except for dancing. Or, as an alternative:
1. Have a knowledge of singing. Have a pleasing voice.
2. Know two Scout songs and be able to sing them, or lead the Scout Troop in singing.

3. Be able to do sight reading.
4. Have a knowledge of note signs and terms.
   Or, as an alternative:
1. Sound correctly on a Bugle the customary army calls of the United States.

28. Naturalist.   (Flower.)

1. Make a collection of fifty species of wild flowers, ferns and grasses and correctly name them. Or,
1. Fifty colored drawings of wild flowers, ferns or grasses drawn by herself.
2. Twelve sketches or photographs of animal life.

29. Needlewoman.   (Scissors.)

1. Know how to cut and fit. How to sew by hand and by machine.
2. Know how to knit, embroider or crochet.
3. Bring two garments cut out by herself; sew on hooks and eyes and buttons.   Make a button-hole.
4. Produce satisfactory examples of darning and patching.

30. Pathfinder.   (Hand.)

1. Know the topography of the city, all the public buildings, public schools, and monuments.
2. Know how to use the fire alarm.
3. In the country know the country lanes and roads and by-paths, so as to be able to direct and guide people at any time in finding their way.

4. Know the distance to four neighboring towns and how to get to these towns.

5. Draw a map of the neighborhood with roads leading to cities and towns.

6. Be able to state the points of the compass by stars or the sun, using watch as compass when sun is invisible.

31. Pioneer. (Axes.)
1. Tie six knots. Make a camp kitchen.
2. Build a shack suitable for three occupants.

32. Photography. (Camera.)
1. Know use of lens, construction of camera, effect of light on sensitive films and the action of developers.
2. Be able to show knowledge of several printing processes.
3. Produce 12 photos of scout activities, half indoor and half outdoors, taken, developed and printed by herself, also 3 pictures of either birds, animals, or fish in their natural haunts, 3 portraits and 3 landscapes.

33. Scribe. (Open Book.)
1. Must present a certificate from teacher of her school, showing a year's record of excellence in scholarship, attendance and deportment.
2. Describe in an article, not to exceed a thousand words, how a newspaper is made; its different departments, the functions of its staff; how the local news is gathered; how the news of the world is gathered and disseminated.

3. Define briefly a news item.
4. Define briefly an editorial.
5. Define briefly a special story.
6. Tell how printer's ink is made.
7. Tell how paper is made.
8. Describe evolution of typesetting from hand composition to machine composition.
9. Write 12 news articles (preferably one a month), not to exceed 500 words each, on events that come within the observation of the Scout that are not public news, as for instance, school athletic events, entertainments of Scouts, church or school, neighborhood incidents.
10. Write a special story on some phase of scoutcraft, a hike, or camping experience, etc.
    Or, as an alternative:
    Write a good poem.
    Write a good story.
    Know principal American authors of prose and verse in the past and present century.

34. Signaling. (Two Flags.)

1. Send and receive a message in two of the following systems of signaling: Semaphore, Morse. Not fewer than twenty-four letters a minute.
2. Receive signals by sound, whistle, bugle or buzzer.
3. Or general service (International Morse Code).

35. Swimmer. (Life-buoy.)

1. Swim fifty yards in clothes, skirt and boots.
2. Demonstrate diving.
3. Artificial respiration.
4. Flinging a life-line.
5. Flinging a life-buoy.
6. Saving the drowning.

Requirements for examination must

be sent to parents of candidate for approval. Approval must also be obtained from the family physician or some other doctor.

36. Telegraphy. (Telegraph Pole.)
    1. Be able to read and send a message in Morse and in Continental Code, twenty letters per minute, or must obtain a certificate for wireless telegraphy. (These certificates are awarded by Government instructors.) (See p. 77.)

Captain's Badge

Part III

GAMES AND ATHLETICS FOR GIRLS

THE finest type of physical vigor is developed from playing vigorous outdoor games. This applies to girls as well as to boys. Games have the great advantage over drills and gymnastics that they are worth while for the fun alone. Play is a necessary and natural activity for every individual. Unless each one of us gives the proper share of her time to wholesome forms of recreation, she cannot be cheerful and happy, and thus she cannot influence those around her toward greater happiness. Each one of us should so plan each day that we shall spend at least one hour playing vigorous games outdoors. The younger girls should use the whole afternoon for play and recreation. No girl can become a normal woman without having had her share of joyful and active play.

Girls nowadays are playing more and more, and growing stronger and more athletic. As a result they have better health and greater beauty. No beauty parlor can produce the perfect complexion and bright eyes which nature gives to the out-of-doors girl.

There are certain cautions which girls should use in practicing games and athletics. After they are twelve or thirteen, they should avoid sports like high or broad jumping, which cause a heavy jar upon landing. Girls should not compete in long distance running, or in games which call for violent and long-continued exertion. Basket-ball may easily be too severe if played according to boys' rules or for long halves. In such games there should be a gradual preparation for the competition. An examination of the heart by a physician is very

desirable, before this type of game is played. Girls frequently overdo rope-skipping. No girl should jump more than fifty times in succession. Excessively keen competition under trying conditions frequently has a bad effect upon girls of a nervous temperament. Of course, girls should rest and not take part in active games when they are physically incapacitated. There are, however, a wide variety of games and sports in which girls may find both pleasure and profit. The ideal type of exercise for girls is found in swimming, walking and similar activities in which the exertion is not excessively violent, and which call for long-continued or repeated efforts. Girls excel in endurance in such sports.

Team games are especially valuable for girls as they need the moral discipline of learning to efface themselves as individuals and to play as a member of the team. That is, they learn to coöperate. Among the team games suitable for girls are: field hockey, soccer, baseball played with a soft ball and basket-ball.

Among athletic events that may be used for girls, are: short sprints, usually not over fifty yards, throwing balls for distance, relay races and balancing competitions.

Walking is a delightful sport when done at a good pace, in the country. All girls are fond of rope-skipping and skating.

Novelty competitions, in wide variety, may easily be invented to amuse a group of Scouts. The following will suggest many other variations: A short walking match, heel and toe. The distance may vary from twenty to one hundred yards or more. The same competition may be conducted going backward.

Have all the girls take a prone position, face downward, hands and feet in a specified position. On a signal, get up and run to the finishing line. The usual signal is "On your marks," "Get set," "Go." There should be no movement whatever until the final signal "Go."

Have the players hop backward or forward in a race. Various combinations of these will readily suggest themselves.

Two or more teams of girls may find much fun in simple passing games. Arrange the teams in line, either seated or standing. Have them pass such an object as a bean bag, ball or stick in a specified way. For instance, if the girls are seated, one behind the other, the bean bag may be passed backward over the right shoulder with one hand, around the back of the last girl, and forward over the left shoulder. The game starts with the bag on the ground in front of the leader, and is finished when the leader replaces it there, after it has passed through the hands of each girl on the team. Be careful to see that there are the same number of girls on each team, and that the lines occupy, when arranged, the same space on the ground. Next let the players pass the bag backward overhead with both hands, and forward in any manner they like.

The following variation will introduce an additional feature that makes the game all the livelier. Let the object be passed back to the last player who then runs forward and takes the place of the leading player, every player in that line moving back one position as this player runs to the front of the line. This is continued until the captain or leader has gone through every place in the line and run back to the front. The team whose captain gets to the front first, wins the game.

Another stage of this game may be played by stretching a cord or rope across in front of the two lines, eight or ten feet high. As each player advances, the bag or ball must be thrown over the rope from the near to the far side, caught, and then thrown back. Any player failing to catch the object must make the throw over again. After she returns to the head of the line, the object is passed back to the last player in the same manner, and the game continues until the captain or leading player has passed through every position in the line, and come back to the front.

A similar game may be played with a basket-ball and basket-ball goals, each girl being required to shoot a goal at one or both ends of the basket-ball court. In the woods or in camp a ring or hoop may be substituted for the basket-ball goal.

Hundreds of such simple games are found in the books on games listed in the Handbook. A few of the more useful and popular games are described below.

Three Deep

Twenty-four or more players form a circle of pairs with space enough between the players (who stand closely one behind the other, facing the center of the circle) to allow the runners to turn and run in all directions. Two players on the outside of the circle and at a distance from each other begin the game. One of these is called the "tagger," the other is "It." She tries to tag "It" before she can secure a place in front of any of the pairs forming the circle. If she succeeds, rôles are changed, the player who has been tagged then becomes the "tagger" and the former "tagger" tries to secure a place in front of some pair. But whenever the runner (the player pursued) has succeeded in getting in front of a pair before being tagged, then the hindmost (the last or third, in the respective rank) must take to her heels and seek to evade the unsuccessful "tagger" who now turns her attention to the new runner. In trying to evade a tagger the successive players may run in any direction, either left or right, outside the circle, but not pass in front of any one rank to another rank in such a manner as to induce wrong starts. A hindmost player may also form in front of his own rank, making the second player in such rank hindmost or "third." The play is always directed against the third or last of a rank, two players being the number limited to each place.

(When classes of players in the beginning are too large the circle may be formed by rows or ranks of threes, instead of twos or pairs.)

Expert players may form several circles and run from circle to circle, two pairs playing simultaneously. The above play may be varied in a number of ways.

Day and Night

The players divide into two parties, form in two lines, back to back, about three paces apart. One of the lines is named the "Day Party" the other the "Night Party." The leader has a disk painted black on one side and white on the other. (A coin may be used instead of the disk.) In front of each party is a goal. The leader throws the disk into the air. If the disk alights with the white side up the leader calls "Day." The "Day Party" then rushes toward its goal and the "Night Party" pursues, tagging as many players of the "Day Party" as possible. These they take back to their own line. The disk is thrown again, and the party whose side turns up starts for their goal as before. The game continues in this way until all the players on one of the sides are lost.

Sculptor

One of the players is chosen as the "Sculptor" and she arranges the other players in different positions and attitudes as statues. No player dares move or speak, for as soon as she does the sculptor punishes her by beating her with a knotted handkerchief or towel (the sack-beetle). After having arranged the players to suit her fancy the sculptor leaves the playground, saying: "The sculptor is not at home." No sooner is she gone than the statues come to life, sing, dance, jump and play havoc in general. On the return of the sculptor she counts, "One, two, three," and any player who is not in her former posture at "Three" receives a beating with the knotted handkerchief from the sculptor. Should the sculptor punish the wrong statue all the players rush at her with knotted handkerchiefs and drive her to a goal previously decided upon, and the game is resumed with some other player as sculptor.

Cross Tag

Any player who is chased may be relieved by any other player running between her and the one trying to tag her. The latter must then run after the player who ran between, till she in turn is relieved.

Dodge Ball

Of any even number of players, half form a circle, while the other half stand inside the ring, facing outward. The players in the center dodge the ball, which, while in play, is thrown by any of those forming the circle. Those who are hit with the ball take their places among those around the circle, and have an equal chance at those remaining in the center. One is put out at a time. This is kept up until no one is left, in the circle, after which the players exchange places, that is, those who were in the circle now form around the circle, and *vice versa*.

Kim's Game

Place twenty or thirty small articles on a tray or table, or the floor, and cover with a cloth—different kinds of buttons, pencils, corks, nuts, string, knives, or other such small things. Make a list and have a column opposite for each player's name. Uncover for just one minute and then take each player by herself and check off the articles she can remember. The winner is the one who remembers the most.

Morgan's Game

Players run quickly to a certain bill-board or shop window where an umpire is posted to time them a minute for their observation. They then run back to head-quarters and report all they can remember of the advertisements on bill-board or objects in shop window.

Scout Meets Scout

Patrols of Scouts are to approach each other from a distance. The first to give the signal that the other is in sight wins. In this game it is not fair to disguise but hiding the approach in any way is admissible. You can climb a tree, ride in any vehicle, or hide behind some slowly moving or stationary object. But be sure to keep in touch with the one who is to give the signal.

It is best that others should not know the Scouts' secret passwords, so one is given at a time in this book for those that can *search best*.

Acting Charades

may be indoors or out. A very good one is for two or three players to act as if they wanted some special thing that is in sight. The first who discovers what this is then selects some other players to act with her.

Unprepared Plays

Relate the plot of some simple play, after which assign a part to each of several to act out. Let them confer for a short time and then act it. This develops many fine talents and is one of the most useful games for the memory, expression, and imagination.

A Scout always shakes hands when she loses a game and congratulates the winner.

INVENTORY GAME. Let each girl go into a room for half a minute and when she comes out let her make a list of what she has seen. Then compare lists to find who has seen the most.

TESTING NOSES. This is easiest with the competitors blindfolded. Let them smell different things and tell what they are. Also the objects may be placed in bags but this means much more work.

CHASING AN OWL. Another good stalking game is chasing the owl. This is done in thick woods where one Scout represents the owl hooting at intervals and then moving to one side for a distance. Each pursuer when seen is called out of the game and the owl, if a real good one, may get safely back to her stump.

TURKEY AND WILDCAT is played by the turkey blindfolded "going to roost" in some place where there are plenty of twigs or dry leaves to crack and rustle. At the first sound the turkey jumps. If not then in reach of the wildcat she is safe and another wildcat has a chance. This is sometimes very laughable for the turkey being blindfolded may jump right on the wildcat.

FAR AND NEAR. On any walk, preferably in patrol formation, let each keep a list of things seen such as birds, flowers, different kinds of trees, insects, vehicles, tracks, or other "sign." Score up in points at the end of the walk on return to the club rooms.

ATHLETIC FEATS

The Palm Spring

Stand at a little distance from a wall with your face toward it and leaning forward until you are able to place the palm of your hand quite flat on the wall; you must then take a spring from the hand and recover your upright position without moving either of your feet. It is better to practice it first with the feet at a little distance only from the wall, increasing the space as you gradually attain greater proficiency in the exercise.

Foot-Throw

Put a basket-ball between your feet in such a manner that it is held between your ankles and the inner side of the feet; then kick up backward with both your feet and in this manner try to jerk the ball over your head, catching it when it comes down.

Hand Wrestling

Two players face each other, feet planted firmly, full stride position apart, right hands grasped. Each player tries to displace the other player. One foot moved displaces a player.

Sitting Toe Wrestle)

Two players sit on a mat facing each other, knees bent perpendicularly, toes touching opponent's. Pass stick under knees and clasp your hands in front of knees. When the signal is given, attempt to get your toes under opponent's toes and upset her.

(An excellent list of games to be used while in camp will be found on page 440 of *Games for the Home, School, and Gymnasium*, by Jessie H. Bancroft. See, also, additional books listed under this topic in the Handbook.)

CAMPING

It is advisable that Patrols or Companies should have some place of their own at which to camp. Some small plot of woodland is easily secured near most any of our cities. At the beaches it is frequently impossible to secure the privacy desirable. The seaside is not easily fenced in. If you own your camping ground all desirable sanitary conditions can be looked after and buildings of a more or less permanent nature erected. Even a "brush house" in a spot which you are allowed to use exclusively is better than having to hunt a place every time you want to camp out. "Gypsying" from place to place is unadvisable.

When you have your own camp, too, much better chances for study will be found possible. You will have your own trees, flowers, and birds to notice and care for, and a record of them is valuable even in a very limited space. Think of the beautiful work of White—*The Natural History of Selborne.*

Name your camp by all means. Long ago we formed the habit of naming all our camps using by preference the name of the first bird seen there. Now we use the Seminole name. So we have our "Ostata" and "Tashkoka." Some of the names are too hard, though, for civilized tongues. "Mooganaga" for instance, might hurt somebody's mouth when she tries to pronounce it.

When going into camp *never* forget matches. When leaving camp I used to put all my spare matches into a dry empty bottle, cork it tight, and hide it. After many years I have found my matches as good as "new" where I had hidden them. By rubbing two sticks together one can make a fire without matches.

Camping out is one of my hobbies. Walks and picnics

are all very well as far as they go, but to get the full benefit of actual contact with Nature it is absolutely necessary
to camp out.   That does not mean sleeping on wet bare
ground but just living comfortably out of doors, where
every breath of heaven can reach you and all wild
things are in easy reach.   A camp can be easily planned
within daily reach of many of our large cities but should
be far enough to escape city sounds and smells.   It is
not a camp, however, if it is where a stream of strangers
can pass by at any time of the day or night within sight
and hearing.

Water is a supreme requisite at any camp.   Water
to swim in may be dispensed with in extreme cases,
but you can't carry your water with you and have
a comfortable time.   I have been where I had to do it
so I know how it is.   Also I have had to dig water out of
the ground.   That is not an easy operation so be sure
and camp near a well or spring.   Wood, too, you will
want and it must be dry.   Don't try to cook with fat
pine.   It's all right to kindle with but not for cooking.
Your bacon fried over it will be as fine eating as a porous
plaster.   Fry your potatoes.   If you must roast them
dig a hole in the ashes and cover them deep.   Then go
away and forget them.   Let some one else come along
and cook all sorts of things on top of them.   When you
come back rake them out of the ashes and astonish every
one.

Be sure your cooking fire is not too big.   You must be
able to get up to it comfortably close without scorching
your face.   Start a small fire and feed it as required with
small dry twigs.   Cooking over an outdoor fire is a fine
art and has to be studied carefully.   It should be called
almost a post-graduate course in the camp studies.   Of
course the regular camp-fire can be made as big and
smoky as you like.   Smoke is fine to watch but not to
breathe.   Even the mosquitoes dislike it.

Roughing it is all very fine to talk about, but it is best

to make your camp as comfortable as possible. The ground is good to sleep upon but not stones and sticks. It's really astonishing how big a stick, no longer than your finger, can grow in one night. Take my word for it and don't try it. It won't pay. A hammock is my preference but a cot is about as good. On a pinch twigs and grass are not to be despised. Moss is apt to be moist but there is no possible objection to clean dry sand.

Be sure not to. let your fire get away from you and spread. Besides the damage to trees and fences that it may do it is impossible to tell what suffering it may cause to animal life. So, be very careful.

To prevent forest fires Congress passed the law approved May 5, 1900, which—

Forbids setting fire to the woods, and
Forbids leaving any fires unextinguished.

When you leave your camp clean up. Fragments of food—not pickles—can be put up somewhere for the birds. At some of our camps we have regular places to feed the birds and they get to know what time to come there. Here in the woods my wrens have established for themselves the hour of sunrise, and it is partly to escape their scolding for neglect that I get up with the sun. Mrs. Jenny scolds furiously but for actual singing she can beat any bird in the woods.

Perhaps you notice that we have said nothing about snakes. Now it is really a very rare thing to see a snake in the woods. You have to look very carefully to find them, for they seem to be about the most timid of all creatures. So far as danger from poisonous snakes is concerned you are in much more danger from the driver of a dray than from a snake. Take our word for

it, snakes are much more afraid of you than you are of
them.   Give them the least little bit of a chance and they
will be out of the way before you can see them.   A gorged
snake—that is one that has just taken a full meal—may be
sluggish but in a majority of cases he will crawl away and
hide in some secure place till the process of digestion is
over.   Do not go near a tub if you are afraid of water for
you can get drowned in it about as easy as you can get
bitten by a snake in the woods and to wind up the subject, not one-tenth of the people who get snake bitten, die
from it.   A very few do die but most of them die from the
bad treatment they receive afterwards.   The "deadly
auto" will not get out of your way but all snakes will.

Once in a while you may find clinging in a low bush
a pretty little green snake.   It will readily submit to being
handled and is perfectly harmless.   We have found these
snakes useful in the house to kill flies.   The harmless
snakes are the brown snake, the common banded moccasin, the black mountain snake, the green snake.   The
garter and ring-necked snakes wear Eve's wedding-ring
as a collar.   They cannot hurt and they eat up quantities
of insects, but beware of the yellow and brown rattle-
snakes, especially after rainy weather, for it is said that
after wet weather they cannot make any noise with their
rattles and therefore you are not warned of their presence.
The most deadly snake, the moccasin, is brownish with
a flat head.

The green lizards, too, will almost rid a house of
flies if left to wander about at will.   The fence lizard,
a scaly alligator looking chap, is just as useful but never
gets tame.

Try petting a toad some time.   He will get to be
quite at home in a garden and pay well, for he will eat all
kinds of destructive insects.   Some gardeners buy toads,
paying as high as a quarter apiece, for they know how
much good they can do.   A toad digs his hole backwards.   Watch him and see the fun.   In the spring if

there is water near he may be induced to sing to you. If you think he is slow and clumsy you have only to see how quick he can catch a fly.

Provisioning a Camp

This should be a matter of mature consideration. Unless there is some place near by where deficiencies can be supplied your camp may be a misery instead of a pleasure. Have lists made out of the things each is to bring, if it is to be a coöperative affair. It may be best to have a committee, even if it is a committee of one, to do all the buying. But even in this case individual tastes must be consulted. A full list should be made out and strictly adhered to. At one camp where each brought what she thought best there were six cans of soup, four pounds of sugar, and no tea or coffee.

Canned goods are all very well if you do not have to carry them too far. So too are potatoes. For lightness on long trips, dried fruits and meal or grits are a wise selection. Oatmeal is light and easy to cook. Prepared batter-cake flour is a pure joy to the camp cook. Once when camping in the mountains we had unexpected difficulties. We were at such an elevation that water boiled at too low a temperature to cook many things "done," so the frying-pan there reigned supreme. As to that same frying-pan be sure to select the "long handled kind." If not you will have to splice out the handle with a long stick. Never pack up your "unwetables" in paper bags. At any time a shower or even a heavy dew at night may make you run short on salt, sugar, or flour. Covered tin cans are too cheap to make it necessary to run any such risks. Have a lantern and oil of course. Candles blow out too easily to be of much use. For sudden calls for a light the pocket electric affair is very good and cheap. Keep it standing up. The batteries waste quite fast if it is left down on the side.

The quantity of provisions to be taken depends on the length of stay. Consult any good military or naval ration list and a very good guess can be made. They all seem to lay stress on beans which certainly are very good if you have the "Boston" appetite.

Keep your camp clean. Keep it in order. Let your motto be, "Tidy as you go." It is as bad to have to hunt for a thing you want in camp as it is at home and particularly exasperating if, when you have found it, you must wash it before using. "A place for everything and that place anywhere" is a bad camp rule, though it does sound as if it was a real easy way of disposing of the matter. Dig a hole to throw slops in and do not let them "fly" on the ground. You may want to sit down right there. Whatever the birds will eat should be put aside for them. All other scraps and things that may become offensive *must* be buried. Don't start to breed flies or fever. When near the water some part of this rule may be dispensed with in favor of the fish and crabs. They may be judiciously baited up, but if you are going to fish for them see that they are not overfed.

There are times and seasons when wild fruits and berries are a most welcome addition to the camp fare, but unless you are perfectly sure of the supply do not reckon on them too much in making up your provision list. Better let them be a sort of joyful surprise. So too of fish and game. "Don't count your chickens before they are hatched." Fresh smilax shoots can scarcely be told from asparagus. Palmetto cabbage well cooked is fine; poorly prepared it is vile. Let some one that knows about these things "do" them for you.

The "gipsy kettle" is picturesque and only picturesque. Drive a stout crotched stake on each side of the fire and put a stout stick across them. Use strong wire hooks—S-shaped on which to hang pots over the fire. If hung through the handle on the stick they are apt to boil over and put out the fire before you know it. They may be quickly lifted from the wire hooks as soon as they begin to look dangerous. Even the coffee-pot may be rigged with a wire handle by which to be hung. Wire and string are our special hobbies in camp. Fan a fire instead of blowing it. Your breath has lost most of its combustible gas. A tin or wooden plate makes a good fan. Put away dry kindling every night. You don't know what sort of weather it will be to-morrow.

Use all precaution against your fire spreading. This is particularly necessary where there are tents. A dry tent will almost "whisk" up in smoke if the fire catches it. Rake dry leaves well away from about the fire. It may be best sometimes to make "a burn" round the camp. Do this a little at a time beating out all traces of the fire in the part burnt over. Be in no hurry about this but be thorough. Leave no smouldering embers or chunks of rotten wood smoking behind you. Burn clean as you go.

Camp Oven

The camp kitchen or camp oven is made with two lines of soda bricks, stones, or thick logs flattened at the top, about six feet long, slightly splayed from each other, being four inches apart at one end and eight inches at the other. The big end should be towards the wind, so that a sort of tunnel is formed in the big end at windward. Start your fire and the draught will carry the heat along the tunnel.

Daily Routine in Camp

Have a set of general orders posted every morning. There should be one officer of the day and one orderly. These will be appointed in turn. The general order should be read before breakfast and include all duties and so far as possible the excursions and games for the day. In appointing cooks and details for the various duties be sure not to work the "willing horse" too hard but let all share as much

*alike as possible. Some will always want to volunteer too
often and some will try to avoid certain duties distasteful
to themselves or "swap" with others. This should not be
allowed but helping must never be barred completely. Inspect camp personally at least once a day and call attention
to shortcomings kindly without chiding. You can help
your girls to help themselves. A "driver" in camp is sure
to breed hard feelings and cause discontent. The camp is
a hard school for the instructor. One of the necessary laws
in a camp is that after lights are out at night, no one must
speak. Silence should reign.*

In some places mosquitoes are very troublesome. Oil
of citronella will drive them away for a time but a
"smudge" may be necessary. They won't stay in
smoke or wind, so hunt the breeze. There are some
other flies just as bad to which the same treatment may
be applied. "Black-flies" of the northern woods are
about the worst insect pest in America, though the mosquitoes in some parts of the South, are nearly as bad. In
some of the coast regions, too, there is a species of "sand-
fly" or midge that is exceedingly annoying, but all of
these are readily controlled by the "smudge." This is
a steady smoke not necessarily of an ill-smelling nature.
One of the very best materials for a "smudge" is green
cedar branches. They need some pretty hot coals to
keep them smouldering but are very effective.

Very few accidents need happen in camp. But still
it may be a wise precaution to go over with each patrol,
before the camping trip, some simple exercise in bandaging and other "First Aid" exercises. In a book of the
scope of this one it is not possible to give a full course of
instruction in such matters, so it seems best to make only
casual mention and leave details to the judgment of the
patrol leaders and captains.

If any boating is to be a part of the program
they should inform themselves carefully which of their

patrol can swim and just how expert they are. **Also** instruct in methods of throwing things to a drowning person or one who has just met with some mishap in a boat—such for instance as losing an oar. A board or a plank should not be thrown toward a person in the water but launched toward them. When adrift in an unmanageable boat cast anchor and wait for assistance. *Never rock a boat for fun*. A Scout who so far forgets herself as to do such a foolhardy act should be forbidden to go into a boat again for some time as a punishment. Most drowning accidents are from some such *fun*. It is *sin*— not *fun*.

When bathing obey strictly all orders regarding distance to be ventured and other rules. You may think they are mere summary restrictions but you are probably not the best judge.

Last summer a party of boys were bathing. Contrary to orders they scattered apart instead of keeping close together. While the Captain's back was turned looking after the smaller boys, some of the big boys began to dare each other to go farther and farther out. When the Captain blew the whistle for them some still persisted in swimming away from the beach and one of them was drowned. And to make it still worse he drowned in shallow water where, if he had only known or had kept his wits about him, he could have waded ashore.

CAMP ORDERS

In going into camp it is essential to have a few "Standing Orders" published, which may be added to from time to time, if necessary. These should be carefully explained to patrol leaders, who should then be held fully responsible for their Scouts carrying them out exactly.

Such orders might point out that each patrol will camp separately from the others, and that there will be a comparison between the respective camps as to cleanliness and good order of tents and surrounding ground.

5 ·

Patrol leaders to report on the good or indifferent work of their Scouts, which will be recorded in the Captain's book of marks.

Bathing should be under strict supervision to prevent non-swimmers getting into dangerous water. No girl must bathe when not well.

Bathing picket of two good swimmers will be on duty while bathing is going on, and ready to help any girl in distress. This picket will be in the boat with bathing costume and overcoat on. They may bathe only when the general bathing is over and the last of the bathers has left the water. If bathing in the surf, a stake should be driven into the sand on the beach and a rope securely fastened to the stake so that non-swimmers can hold on to the rope in the water.

Orders as to what is to be done in case of fire alarm.

Orders as to boundaries, grounds to be worked over, damages to fences, property, good drinking water, etc.

No Scout allowed out of bounds without leave.

No lads allowed inside bounds without leave.

Camping Equipment Necessary for One Week or Longer

1 Transport wagon.
2 Tents for girls.
1 Tent for officer.
3 Mallets and sufficient tent-pegs.
2 Blankets for each Scout.
2 Blankets for officer.
1 Kit bag each (2 ft. by 1 ft. or bigger).
8 Waterproof ground sheets.
3 Buckets.
3 Hurricane lamps.
2 Balls of twine (medium).
1 Spade.
1 Hatchet.

Kitchen Equipment

Bowls.
2 Saucepans.
1 Large frying pan.
Kettle.
Gridiron.
Butcher knife.
Kitchen fork.
Spoons, ladles, and tea strainer.
Six tea cloths.
Cleaning rags.
Chopping board and knife.
Kitchen soap and scouring powder.
1 Dish pan.

Clothing and Equipment for Each Scout

1 Set of underwear, cotton flannel nightgown, and lisle or cotton stockings for each week. Do not take silk stockings.
1 Dress besides Scout uniform.
1 Pair heavy shoes.
1 Pair rubbers.
3 Handkerchiefs.
1 Apron.
1 Sweater or coat.
Hairbrush and comb and tooth-brush.
3 Towels.
Haversack.
2 Pillow-cases.
Soap and wash rag or sponge.
Bathing suit.
1 Plate.
1 Cup and saucer.
"Hussif" fitted with needles, thread, scissors.

Paper pad and envelopes and pencil.
Knife and fork.
Teaspoon and large spoon.
2 Woolen blankets.

SCOUTCRAFT

Useful Knots

Everyone should be able to tie knots. A knowledge of knots is useful in every trade or calling, and forms an important part of a Girl Scout's training.

As it may happen some day that a life may depend on a knot being properly tied you ought to know the proper way.

THE BOWLINE is a loop that will not slip after the first grip. First make a loop, then pass the end up through it, round the back of the standing part, and down through the loop again. It is often used as a halter for horses.

THE RUNNING BOWLINE. This is the nautical slip knot. First make the loop as in the ordinary bowline but allow a good length of end (A). Pass it round the standing part and up through the loop, and continue as in the ordinary bowline.

THE REEF KNOT. It is used to join two dry ropes of the same thickness. It will not slip, and can be easily untied when wanted. Do not confuse it with the "Granny" knot. It is the *only* knot used in First Aid work.

THE CLOVE HITCH is made with two half-hitches. When fastened to a pole and pulled tight it can slip neither up nor down. Greatly used in pioneering work.

THE HALF-HITCH. Pass the end round a pole, then round the standing part, then through below itself again.

*Sheet Bend.

Middleman's Knot.

Overhand Loop Knot.

Round Turn and
Two Half-Hitches.

*Sheep Shank.

Slip Knot.

*Reef Knot.

*Clove Hitch.

*Fisherman's Knot.

*Bowline.

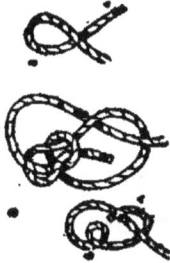

Running Bowline.

Half Hitch.

THE FISHERMAN'S KNOT. Make this knot by tying a simple knot on rope B with the end of rope A, then tie a similar knot on rope A with the end of rope B. Pull the standing parts and the knots will remain fast.

ROUND TURN AND TWO HALF-HITCHES. It is used for making fast a rope so that the strain will not jamb hitches.

THE SHEET BEND. Used for uniting two dry ropes of different thicknesses. First form a loop, then pass the end of the other rope up through the loop, round the back of the end and standing part of loop, and through below itself.

THE SHEEP-SHANK. A Scout should never cut rope unless absolutely necessary. To shorten a guy rope on tent or marquee, gather the rope in the form of two long loops and pass a half-hitch over each loop. It remains firm under a good strain and can be easily undone when required.

MIDDLEMAN'S KNOT. Somewhat similar to the fisherman's knot but in this case only one rope is used. Can safely be used as a halter.

THE SLIP KNOT. You sometimes want to release a knot quickly so this knot is used. It is simply the reef knot with one of the ends (A) pushed through one of the loops. To release, pull end A.

OVERHAND LOOP KNOT. When pulling a rope you may wish to gain more purchase on it or you may wish to insert a short stick to pull with. Use the loop knot shown in our diagram.

IMPORTANT. Many of the knots shown on these pages are open so that you may more easily see their working. but when in use they should always be drawn taut.

The Mariner's Compass

Boxing the compass consists in enumerating the points beginning with north and working around the circle as follows:

North
North by East
North, Northeast
Northeast by North
Northeast
Northeast by East
East, Northeast
East by North
East
East by South
East, Southeast
Southeast by East
Southeast
Southeast by South
South, Southeast
South by East
South

South by West
South, Southwest
Southwest by South
Southwest
Southwest by West
West, Southwest
West by South
West
West by North
West, Northwest
Northwest by West
Northwest
Northwest by North
North, Northwest
North by West
North

How to Read a Map

Conventional Signs & Lettering Used in Field Sketching

Conventional Signs enable you to give information on

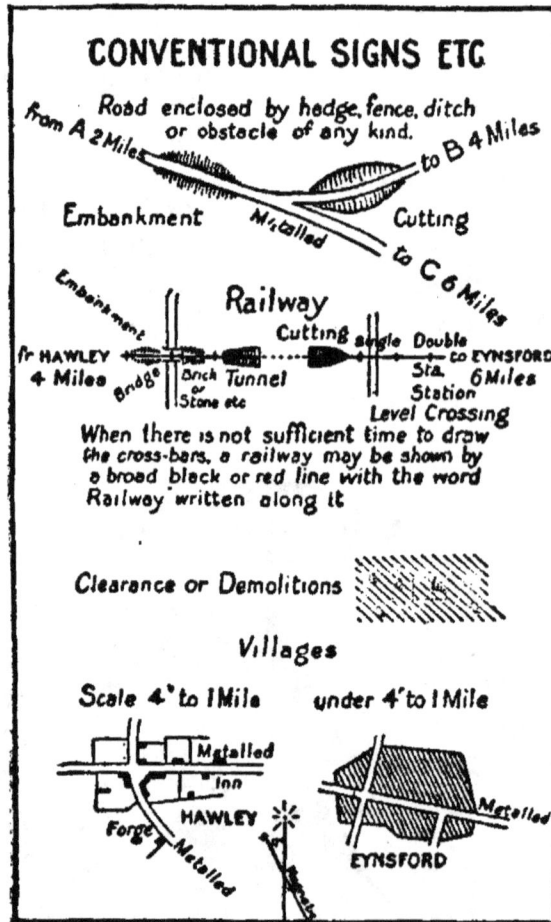

a sketch or map in a simple manner which is easily understood. In addition to the sign it is often necessary to give an additional description, *e. g.*, whether a railway is double or single, the width of roads, the nature of woods (oak, pine, etc.), etc.

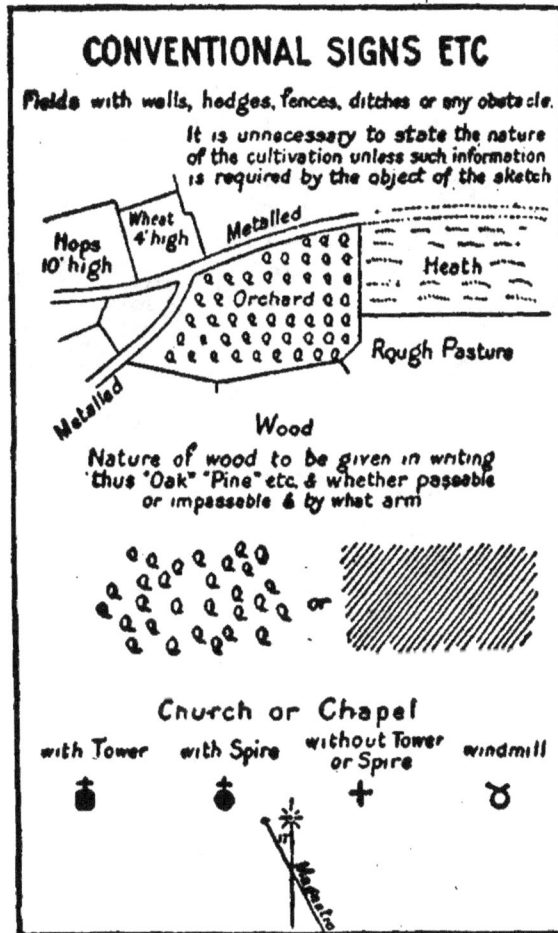

CONVENTIONAL SIGNS ETC

Fields with walls, hedges, fences, ditches or any obstacle.

It is unnecessary to state the nature of the cultivation unless such information is required by the object of the sketch

Hops 10' high

Wheat 4' high

Metalled

Heath

Orchard

Rough Pasture

Metalled

Wood

Nature of wood to be given in writing thus "Oak" "Pine" etc. & whether passable or impassable & by what arm

or

Church or Chapel

with Tower   with Spire   without Tower or Spire   windmill

Whatever lettering is used should be legible and not interfere with the detail of the sketch. All lettering should be horizontal, except the names of roads, railways, rivers, and canals, which should be written along them.

Remember to fill in the North point on your sketch,

as it is useless without it. Leave a margin of about **an** inch all round your sketch and state the scale that **you** have made your sketch, *e. g.*, two inches to the mile.

CONVENTIONAL SIGNS ETC

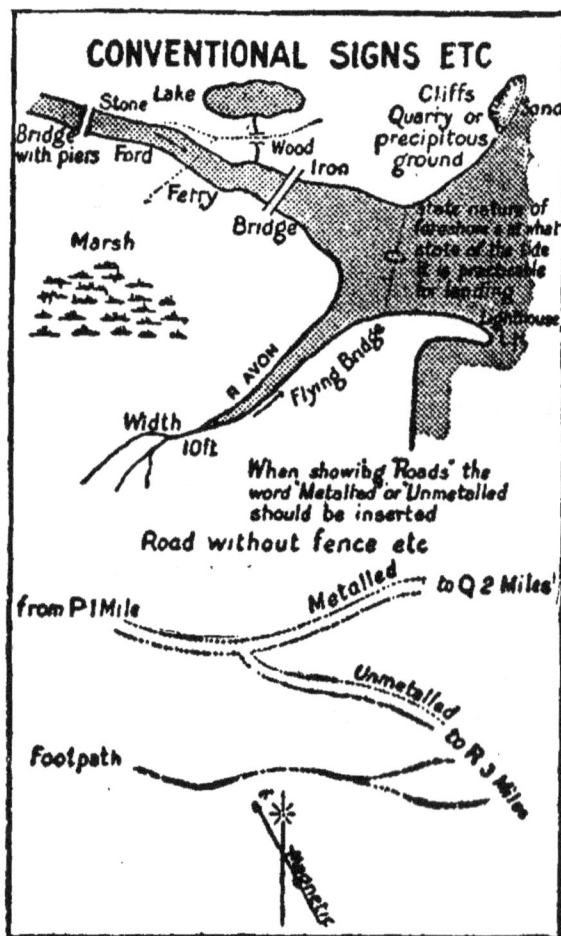

Obstacles

Entrenchments

ABBREVIATIONS

P .... Post Office
T .... Telegraph
S.P. .... Sign Post
W .... Well

Telegraph

SIGNALLING

CONTINENTAL

Used on Submarine Cables, Wireless
and in Foreign Countries

A · —
B — · · ·
C — · — ·
D — · ·
E ·
F · · — ·
G — — ·
H · · · ·
I · ·
J · — — —
K — · —
L · — · ·
M — —
N — ·
O — — —
P · — — ·
Q — — · —
R · — ·
S · · ·
T —
U · · —
V · · · —
W · — —
X — · · —
Y — · — —
Z — — · ·

1 · — — — —
2 · · — — —
3 · · · — —
4 · · · · —
5 · · · · ·
6 — · · · ·
7 — — · · ·
8 — — — · ·
9 — — — — ·
0 — — — — —

Period .... · · · · · ·
Comma .... · — · — · —
Interrogation ..... · · — — · ·
Colon .... — — — · · ·
Semi-colon .... — · — · — ·
Quotation Marks .. · — · · — ·

The letter A is used for the word "Error"
  "   "   K "   "   "   "   "   "Negative"
  "   "   L "   "   "   "   "   "Preparatory"
  "   "   N "   "   "   "   "   "Annulling"
  "   "   O "   "   "   "   "   "Interrogatory"
  "   "   P "   "   "   "   "   "Affirmative"
  "   "   R "   "   "   "   "   "Acknowledgment"

The Morse Code of Signals is not hard to learn but it requires much practice to "receive" even when the message is sent slowly. The old-fashioned instruments were fitted with a ribbon on which the dots and dashes were recorded, but all modern operators depend on the ear.

The code is as follows:

The American Morse Telegraph Alphabet

NUMERALS

Punctuation

Comma, • ▬ • ▬	Exclamation, ▬ ▬ ▬
Semicolon, Si	Parenthesis, Pn
Colon, Ko	Brackets, Bn
Period, • • ▬ ▬ • •	Dollar mark, Sx
Interrogation, ▬ • • ▬ •	Dash, Dx
Quotation, Qn	Hyphen, Hx
Paragraph, ▬ ▬ ▬ ▬	Underline, Ux

Signals

4. Start me.
5. Have you anything for me?
9. Train order (or important military message) — give away.
13. Do you understand?

All sorts of changes may be made when the signals are committed to memory. Flags—up for a dot and side for a dash is one of the commonest and easiest for the beginner; or whistles—long and short blasts: Even the hand or a hat may be substituted; coughing, stamping, and scratching with the foot or a bit of stick. In fact endless changes may be invented for use with this Code.

COMMANDS AND SIGNALS

For the use of the Girl Scouts the following list of words of command and whistle signals has been compiled.

Commands

"Fall in" (in line).
"Alert" (stand up smartly).
"Easy" (stand at ease).
"Sit easy" (sit or lie in ranks).
"Dismiss" (break off).
"Right" or "Left" (turn accordingly).

"Patrol right or patrol left" (patrol in line wheels).
"Quick march" (step off with the left foot first).
"Double" (run with arms down).
"Scouts' pace" (walk fifty paces and run fifty paces alternately).

Whistle Signals

1. One long blast means "Silence," "Alert," "Listen for next signal."

2. A succession of long slow blasts means "Go out," "Get farther away," or "Advance," "Extend," "Scatter."

3. A succession of quick short blasts means "Rally," "Close in," "Come together," "Fall in."

4. Alternate short and long blasts mean "Alarm," "Look out," "Be ready," "Man your alarm posts."

5. Three short blasts followed by one long one from the Captain calls up the patrol leaders.

Any whistle signal must be instantly obeyed at the double as fast as you can run, regardless of anything you may be doing.

By previous agreement many other signals may be arranged. It all depends on the exigencies to be met or the special order or information to be conveyed. But these few important signals should be strictly adhered to in all drills and exercises of Scouts. The compiler of the present volume thinks it unwise to print the secret words so they are left for the patrol leaders and Captain to communicate verbally.

Hand Signals

"ADVANCE" "FORWARD"	Swing the arm from rear to front, below the shoulder.
"RETIRE"	Circle the arm above the head.
"HALT"	Raise the arm to full extension above head.

"DOUBLE"   The closed fist moved **up and down** between your shoulder and thigh.

"QUICK TIME"   To change from the "Double" to the "Quick Time," raise the hand to **the** shoulder.

"REINFORCE"   Swing the arm from the rear to **the** front above the shoulder.

"LIE DOWN"   With the open hand make two or **three** slight movements towards **the** ground.

"WHEEL"   Extend your arm in line with **your** shoulder and make a circular movement in the direction required.

"INCLINE"   Extend your arm in line with **your** shoulder and make a turn with **your** body in the direction required.

Indian Signs

Burnt sticks are placed at the last camp-fire to tell **the** direction the Indians have gone from this spot. Two of them always make a V point and if the third is laid at the point of the V it means north. Across the open end of the V̄ it means south. At one side | V it means east **and** V | would mean west. Now the above mark as made to indicate south would really mean southwest, if **the** stick which indicates direction were a little way to **the** west side—V⁻. Northwest would be V＿.

V   North

V̱   South

|V   East

V| West

V⁻   Southwest

V＿   Northwest

Scout Signs.

Sign.	Secret Patrol or Troop Sign.	Meaning.
→		Road to be followed.
▭→		Letter hidden 3 paces from here in direction of arrow.
✕		This path not to be followed.
⊙		"I have gone home."
⟩✕⟨		War or trouble about.
⟩⟩⟩		Peace.
⌢ (stones)		We camped here because one of us was sick.
◉→		A long way to good water, go in direction of arrow.
◉←		Good water not far in this direction.
◉		This is good water.
🦊↓ 2 G W.		Signature of Scout No. 4 of the Fox Patrol, 21st Glasgow.

Shaking a blanket: I want to talk to you.
Hold up a tree-branch: I want to make peace.
Hold up a weapon (axe) means war: I am ready to fight.
Hold up a pole horizontally, with hands on it: I have found something.

Self-Defense

SHOOTING

All Scouts should know how to shoot. By this we do not mean that you should go all day behind some big dog and try to kill the birds he finds for you, for that is the most useless form of shooting, all things considered, that can be devised. What we mean is that Scouts should know how to load and fire a gun or other firearm so as

6

not to be at a loss for a means of defense should an emergency arise. It is one of the best means to "be prepared." Our preference for practice of this kind is a small rifle as it is less dangerous than any form of pistol and it affords excellent training for hand and eye. Avoid, however, the very high power modern firearms—that kind that "shoot to-day and kill next week," as there is too much danger of reaching some one that is out of sight. The same may be said of the automatic pistol which fills too large a circle with missiles of sudden death.

ARCHERY

The bows and arrows of our ancestors are not to be despised as a means of training hand and eye. Archery is excellent practice for the eye, and good exercise for the muscles. It makes no noise, does not disturb game or warn the enemy. Scouts should know how to shoot with bows and arrows, and they can make them for themselves. The arrow, twenty-six inches long, must be as "straight as an arrow" and tipped with a heavy head, with wings to keep it level. Ash wood is the best. The bow should be unstrung when not in use, or it will get bent. It is usually made your own height. Old gloves should be worn.

STARS

How to Find the Time by the Stars

FIG. 1 shows the stars around the northern pole of the heavens (Pole Star), and the Pointers of the Great Bear, which direct us to the Pole Star.

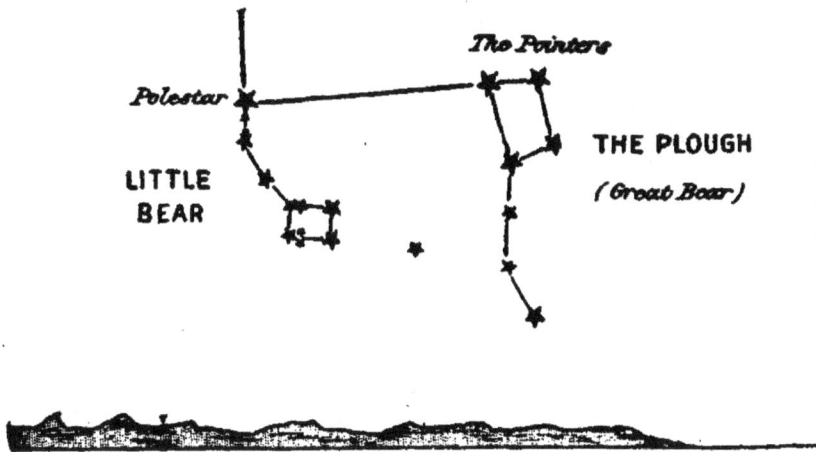

FIG. 1.

Since all stars appear to rise in the East and set in the West (which is really due to our earth turning round under them), the Pointers revolve once around the Pole Star in the opposite direction to the hands of a clock, once in twenty-four hours, or they swing through a quarter of a circle once in six hours; it is thus a simple matter after a little practice to judge what part of the imaginary circle they will pass through in an hour or less.

Assuming that all the stars rise four minutes earlier each night, and that the Pointers of the Plough are vertically above the Pole at midnight at the end of February, we may calculate the position of the Pointers for any hour of the night.

The First Twenty Stars in Order of Brightness

		Date of rising at 9 P.M. in the East.
1.	Sirius, the Dog-star	Dec. 4
2.	(Canopus, of the Ship)	
3.	(Alpha, of the Centaur)	
4.	Vega, of the Lyre.	April 1
5.	Capella, of the Charioteer	Aug. 21
6.	Arcturus, of the Herdsman	Feb. 20
7.	Rigel, of Orion	Nov. 4
8.	Procyon, the Little Dog-star.	Nov. 27
9.	(Achernar, of Eridanus)	
10.	(Beta, of the Centaur)	
11.	Altair, of the Eagle	May 26
12.	Betelgeux, of Orion's right shoulder . . .	Oct. 30
13.	(Alpha, of the Southern Cross)	
14.	Aldebaran, of the Bull's right eye . . .	Oct. 2
15.	Pollux, of the Twins	Nov. 4
16.	Spica, of the Virgin	Mar. 1
17.	Antares, of the Scorpion	May 9
18.	Fomalhaut, of the Southern Fish . . .	Aug. 27
19.	Deneb, of the Swan	Apr. 22
20.	Regulus, of the Lion	Jan. 1

Orion

Then there is another set of stars representing a man wearing a sword and a belt, named "Orion." It is easily recognized by the three stars in line, which are the belt, and three smaller stars in another line, close by, which are the sword. Then two stars to right and left below the sword are his feet, while two more above the belt are his shoulders, and a group of three small stars between them make his head.

Now the great point about Orion is that by him you can always tell which way the North or Pole Star lies, and which way the South, as you can see him whether you are in the South or the North part of the world. The Great Bear can be seen only when you are in the North, and the Southern Cross when you are in the South.

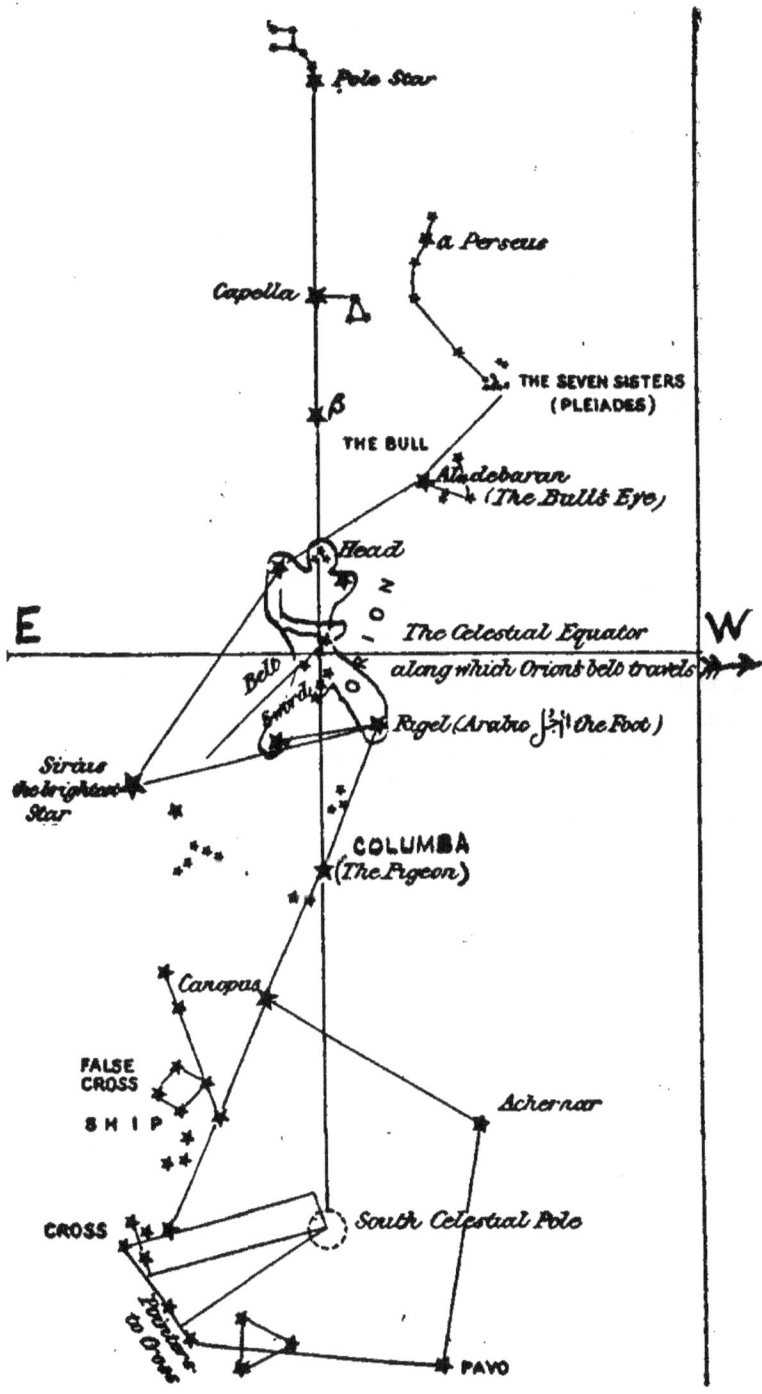

Pole Star

a Perseus

Capella

THE SEVEN SISTERS
(PLEIADES)

β

THE BULL

Aldebaran
(The Bull's Eye)

Head

ORION

E

The Celestial Equator

W

along which Orion's belt travels

Belt

Sword

Rigel (Arabic β' the Foot)

Sirius
the brightest
Star

COLUMBA
(The Pigeon)

Canopus

FALSE
CROSS

Achernar

SHIP

CROSS

South Celestial Pole

Pointers
to Cross

PAVO

If you draw a line by holding up your staff against the sky, from the center star of Orion's belt through the center of his head, and carry that line on through two big stars till it comes to a third, that third one is the North or Pole Star.

Then if you draw a line the other way, beginning again with the center star of the belt, and passing through the center star of the sword, your line goes through another group of stars shaped like the letter L.   And if you go about as far again past L, you come to the South Pole, which unfortunately is not marked by any star. Roughly Orion's sword, the three small stars, points North and South.

East and West.   Orion sets due west, and rises due east, so that, if you can catch him rising or setting, you know where the points of the compass are.   Constellations, such as Orion, or the Bull, rise in the east, four minutes earlier each succeeding night—that is about half an hour earlier every Saturday.

Read *The Song of the Fifty Stars* by Arthur A. Carey, and try to find each star on a chart and then in the Heavens.

The Song of the Fifty Stars

Alpherat, Caph, and Algenib—three leading stars—
Move in front of all the host,
Turning from East to West,
Over the rounded dome;
And, near the head of the line, the Star of the North,
Polaris, turns his round and marks the hub of the wheel.

From Alpherat, North and East, Andromeda shoots,
Like a branch, with Mirach and Almach; while, far in the
    South,
Achernar shines, a beacon-light, at the "End of the
    River."

From Almach pass to Algol, of the changing face,
Called by the Arabs the Demon—
The Medusa of the Greeks.

But, not so fast! lest we forget the little changing star
Whose place is West of Algol, farther South—
Mira, "the Wonderful," in Cetus or the Whale.

Algol leads to Mirfach, the brightest star of Perseus,
Who saved the captive Andromeda, daughter of Cepheus,
    "the Monarch,"
And royal Cassiopeia.

Then comes, surrounded by her sisters, gentle Alcyone,
The peaceful, daughter of the King who rules the tem-
    pestuous winds;
And, running in pursuit of these—the happy Pleiades—
Aldebaran, "the Follower," shines from the eye of the
    Bull.

Next comes Capella—the Mother Goat—watching her
    three Kids;
Her yellow light the color of our Sun.

Capella and Rigel move in line, and afterwards comes
    Nath,
Who marks the horn of the butting Bull.

Orion, the Hunter, on the Equator—the Giant of the
    Arabs—
Shines glorious North and South;
Bellatrix his left shoulder; Mintaka marks his belt.

After Mintaka comes Betelgeux, right shoulder of Orion;
While, between them in order, though farther North,
Is Zeta of Taurus, the Bull, who marks the other horn.

The next is Menkalinan, the shoulder of the Charioteer;
And, two degrees to the Eastward, the Circle of the
    Solstice passes by.
While, far down in the South,
Canopus gleams from the stern of Argo, the Ship.

Sirius, Star of the Greater Dog, brightest of all in the
    heavens,
Is followed by Castor, one of the Twins.
While Procyon—"Dog-in-advance"—the bright "fore-
    runner" of Sirius,
Is followed by Pollux, the greater of the Twins.

Next Regulus comes in the Lion's heart, Denebola, the
    tip of his tail;
While, between them in order, Merak and Dubhe, the
    pointers,
Point to their aim in the North.

Two brilliant stars in the Southern Cross are Alpha and
    Beta Crucis,
The former a glorious double Sun, with a third star in
    attendance;
To see them ourselves we must travel far,
But we know that the glory is great in the South,
Although from us it is hidden.

Next, in the hand of the Virgin, the pointed Ear of
    Wheat—
Spica of the Romans—
Not far from the Autumn Equinox.

Now, back to the North we go, and look for Mizar and
    Alcor—
The Indian Squaw with the little papoose on her back,
And the tip of the tail of the Greater Bear
Where Benetnasch commands.

Now, again to the South, where the forefeet of the
    Centaur
Are marked by Beta and Alpha;—the former is known as
    Hadar—"the Ground";—
The latter sun is nearest to ours
And famous as Serk-t, toward whom the ancient Egyp-
    tians
Turned their temples in homage—

And, between them in order, the great and distant
    Arcturus
Shines out warm in the North.

Pulcherrima—most beautiful—must be sought by those
    who love her;
For she is modest and shy in the presence of the Great
    One.

Nearby is Gemma, the Bud,
In the beautiful Northern Crown.

Near the point where the "roof-tree" crosses the Zodiac
    Ring
Is a warm, red star in Scorpio.
This is Antares; while, in the North,
Etanin marks the Dragon's head.

Mu Sagitarii—closer still to the Solstice and Ecliptic—
Marks the northern part of the heavenly Archer's bow.

On summer evenings, high above our heads,
Vega shines with cool and brilliant light;
While, to the South and East, is Altair of the Eagle.

Nearby is the Northern Cross, or Cygnus,
Whom we call "the Swan,"
With Deneb Adige marking her outspread tail.

The nose of Pegasus, the soaring horse,
Shines out in the star Enif, or Epsilon of Pegasus—a
    triple star—
While Fomalhaut gleams in the South,
Guarding the Fish's Mouth.

Now Scheat and Markab, hand in hand, watch for the
    stragglers—
Bringing up the rear of all the Fifty Stars that have
    passed by.

The Sun Clock

When you have been able to find the North Star it
will be very easy to set up a sun-dial.   This device is not
so valuable now as standard time is universally used.   If
you know the difference between "sun time" and standard time, the sun-dial can be referred to with a fair
amount of accuracy and many people regard it as a
curiosity.

Select a place where the sun shines all day and the
ground is level.   Set up a post or stake perpendicular
and firm.   At night go and "sight" a straight stick at
the North Star and fasten it securely.   This stick will
now be parallel to the axis of the earth and its shadow will
fall at the same line on any given hour no matter what
season of the year it may be.   At noon by the sun the
shadows of the slanting stick and the upright one will
coincide.   This gives you the "sun noon" and the time
by a standard watch or clock will tell you what correction
to apply to your dial to convert its time into standard.
Having once established the noon, or "no hour" mark the
I, II, III, IV, V, and VI with stakes.   Then calculate the
correct sun time of VI A.M. by your standard watch and
stake out the morning hours.   Halves and even quarters
can be marked between if you wish.

A flower dial can be made by having your upright

post a pretty tall one, say ten or even twenty feet, and planting rows of flowers like spokes of a wheel along the hour lines. It may be possible even to select such as are likely to open at or near the indicated hour. The entire semicircle of pegs will also make a pretty finish with tall ornamental foliage plants or shrubs.

PRACTICE

Make a sun-dial on the ground, mark the hours with stor.es or sticks, and see if it shows the time every day.

AMONG THE STARS

Scouts must be able to find their way by night, but unless they practise it they are very apt to lose themselves. At night distances seem much greater, and land-marks are hard to see.

When patrolling in dark places, keep closer together, and in the dark or in the woods or caves keep in touch with each other by catching hold of the end of the next Scout's staff.

The staff is also useful for feeling the way.

WINTER EVENINGS.—*Cut out a quantity of little stars from stamp edging. Take an old umbrella, open, and stick the stars inside it, in the patterns of the chief constellations, then hold it overhead, and turn it once round for twenty-four hours, making the stars rise in the east.*

The sun and the moon appear almost the same size as a rule. When we are a little nearer the sun, in winter, he looks a trifle larger than the moon.

To study the constellations, go out when the stars are bright, armed with a star map and a bicycle lamp to read it by, and spread a rug on the ground to lie on, or have a deck-chair, or hammock. Watch for meteors in August and November.

Let each girl try to draw a sketch map of a given constellation, from memory.

GARDENING

Now what about the gardens, for it goes without saying that Girl Scouts must have gardens. Getting right down and smelling the fresh soil is good for any one. It is mother earth's own breath. Watching the growth of our seeds is a veritable joy of joys. But what had we better plant? Why not let every one plant at least one tree? Never mind what kind of a tree. We will talk about that in a minute but decide at the outset that you will have at least one tree growing this year. Your trees will be a legacy to posterity, a gift from the Girl Scouts to their country. For in this United States of ours we have cut down too many trees and our forests are fast following the buffalo. Nay, the bare face of the land has already begun to prove less attractive to the gentle rains of heaven and offers far too open a path to the raw blasts of winter. In many sections of our country the climate is drier and colder than it was before so much of the forest was destroyed. We are just waking up to this sad fact which it will take many years to rectify. So let us plant trees.

A tree is a tree anyway be it large or small. Some are useful food producers while others are of value for ornament or timber. All are good. There are no bad trees. So if you plant and raise a tree there can be no mistake. Whatever kind you select you will have done well. Fruit and nut trees will of course appeal most strongly to the young, especially to those with good healthy appetites. Many very young trees can be made to return some fruit in a comparatively short time by being budded or grafted. Scouts should learn how to bud and graft. It is not hard. Pears, plums, figs, and peaches all do well in the South as do also some apples and grapes. Peach trees though are in the main short-lived. But trees of different kinds can be grown all over the country. Apples and pears are at their best in the

North and many kinds are very long-lived trees. There are apple trees known to be a hundred years old still bearing. Sugar maple does well where there are long winters, and a wood of them—locally called a "sugar bush"— is a paying piece of property. Most fruit trees are best bought from dealers or obtained from your friends. They do not come "true," as it is called, from the seed. A Baldwin apple-seed will not produce a Baldwin apple. But as all the varieties are got by selecting from seedlings we can experiment if we wish. We are already saving apple-seeds for next year, and it will certainly be grand if we can get a new kind of apple and name it the Girl Scout.

We shall not make many suggestions about flowers. Any and all kinds of flowers will do in your gardens but do not neglect our own wild ones. Take the goldenrod for instance. The finest we have ever seen is grown in a city garden. Many other of our wild flowers will bear cultivating and some well repay the care necessary to "tame" them. The atamasco lily seems to be perfectly at home in the garden and so does the bloodroot. Violets of course would be favorites if our native species were not with one exception scentless. As any gardener's book will tell you all about our "tame" flowers it is not necessary to say much about them.

Part IV

SANITATION

GIRL SCOUTS should do everything in their power to make and keep their homes healthy as well as happy.

Most of you cannot choose your own dwelling, but whether you live in a house, a cottage, a flat, in rooms, or even in one room of a house, you can do a very great deal to keep it healthy and pure.

Fresh air is your great friend; it will help you to fight disease better than anything else. Open all your windows as often as you can, so that the air may get into every nook and corner. Never keep an unused room shut up. You know what a stagnant pool is like—no fresh water runs through it, it is green and slimy, and full of insects and dead things; you would not care to bathe in it. Well, still and stuffy air in a house is very much worse, only, unluckily, its dangers cannot be seen, but they are there lying in ambush for the ignorant person. Disease germs, poisonous gases, mildew, insects, dust, and dirt have it all their own way in stale, used-up air.

You do not like to wash in water other people have used, but it is far worse to breathe air other people have breathed. Air does not flow in and flow out of the same opening at the same time any more than water does, so you want two openings in a room—an open window to let the good air in, and a fireplace and chimney to let the stale air out, or, where there is no fireplace, a window open both at top and bottom. The night air in large towns is purer than the day air, and both in town and country you should sleep with your window open if you want to be healthy. Draughts are not good, as they carry away the heat from your

94

body too fast; so if your bed is too near the window, put up a shelter between it and the open window, and cover yourself more. At least one window on a staircase or landing should always be kept open, and also the larder and the closet windows.

Tidiness

Motto: "TIDY AS YOU GO."

Half your time will be saved if little things are kept tidy. Have a place for everything, and have everything in its place. If you are not sure which is the right place for a thing, think *"Where, if I wanted it, should I go to look for it?"* That place is the right one. Get into the habit of always making hanks of any string you get, and keep them.

War must be waged against rats and mice, or they will multiply and loot everything. If you have no mouse-traps, put a newspaper over a pail of water, break a hole slightly in the center in the form of a star, and place a bit of herring or cheese on the center tips of star to entice the mouse. Let the paper reach to the floor, not too upright, for the mouse to climb up. Try putting broken camphor into their holes; they dislike the smell. Fly and wasp traps are made by tying paper over a tumbler half-filled with water and beer or treacle. Break a hole in the paper, and fit in a tube of rolled paper about one inch long and one inch across.

Try to keep yourself neat, and see that the house you live in is clean, sweet, and pleasant.

GOLDEN HEALTH HABITS FOR GIRL SCOUTS
Contributed by Dr. Thomas D. Wood.

1. Remember Fresh Air and Sunlight Are The Best Medicines.

Ventilate, therefore, every room you occupy. Germs cannot live more than a few minutes in sunlight. Breathe deeply, sleep out, if you can. Work and play as much as possible out-of-doors.

2. Be Not The Slave of Unhygienic Fashions.

Be proud to have efficient feet. Wear light, loose and porous, but sufficient clothing.

3. Eat Slowly.

Do not eat between meals. Chew food thoroughly. Do not overeat. Remember a Girl Scout is always cheerful and helpful. She eats what is provided and is thankful for it. (She does not complain about her food.) If there are any suggestions she can make, she reserves them until mother or the (camp) cook is preparing the menu or the meal. Eat some hard, some bulky and some raw foods.

4. Drink Pure Water at Frequent Intervals.

Remember that not all water that looks pure is free from disease germs. Boil the water if the Scout leader (or older person) is doubtful about it. The few minutes spent in boiling and cooling water is time well spent. Do not drink water when there is food in the mouth.

5. Be Mistress of Your Time—Be Regular in Your Habits of Life.

Go to bed early enough to get sufficient sleep. Be in bed 10½ to 10 hours each night. Get up in the morning promptly. Do not doze after it is time to get up. If you have not had enough sleep go to bed earlier the next night.

Be sure your bowels move regularly, at least once a day. If outside engagements are so pressing as to conflict with your personal health, remember you have an important "previous engagement" with yourself for sufficient time for meals, sleep, out-of-door exercise and, if necessary, rest.

6. Avoid Infection and Do Not Spread It.

Wash your hands always before eating. Use your handkerchief to cover a sneeze or cough and try to avoid coughing, sneezing or blowing the nose in front of others, or at the table. Do not use a common towel or drinking cup, or other appliance which may contain disease germs.

7. Keep Clean.

The smell of flowers has been said to be their soul. Try to keep your body as fresh as possible with the sweetness of cleanliness, not perfumery. Take a sponge bath, shower or quick tub bath daily.

8. Play Hard and Fair.

Be loyal to your team mates and generous to your opponents.

Study hard—and in work, study or play, do your best.

9. Remember Dentist's Bills are Largely Your Own Fault.

Get the habit of cleaning your teeth and rinsing your mouth after each meal. It is more than worth the habit.

10. Remember Silence Is Golden.

In solitudes poets and philosophers have touched the heights of life. It is valuable for everyone to take account of stock occasionally with oneself.

HEALTH

Exercises and their Object

THE best results of exercise are to be had outdoors from the activity of vigorous games. Some of us are so placed that we cannot have daily recreation outdoors and it becomes necessary to give our bodies some type of activity to keep them normal. More than half the weight of the body is made up of muscular tissue. If this muscle is not used the health of the whole body is affected. Exercise is a necessary condition of health, just as food and sleep are. The body is very responsive to the demands made upon it. In fact, each one of us can mold her own body, very much as a sculptor fashions a statue. This is done by giving the body proper care and the right forms of activity. A weak, infirm physique is nothing less than a crime. It is the duty of each one of us, both for our own sakes, and for the benefit of future generations, to perfect our physical frame. It is a duty to be strong and beautiful in body as well as in mind and spirit.

The Nose

Always breathe through the nose. Fifty years ago Mr. Catlin wrote a book called *Shut your Mouth and Save your Life*, and he showed how the Red Indians for a long time had adopted that method with their children to the extent of a cruel habit of tying up their jaws at night, to ensure breathing through the nostrils.

Breathing through the nose prevents germs of disease getting from the air into the throat and stomach; it also prevents a growth in the back of the throat called "adenoids," which reduce the breathing capacity of the nostrils, and also cause deafness.

By keeping the mouth shut you prevent yourself from

getting thirsty when you are doing hard work. The habit of breathing through the nose prevents snoring. Therefore practice keeping your mouth shut and breathing through your nose.

Ears

A Scout must be able to hear well. The ears are very delicate, and once damaged are apt to become incurably deaf. No sharp or hard instrument should be used in cleaning the ear. The drum of the ear is a very delicate, tightly stretched skin which is easily damaged. Very many children have had the drums of their ears permanently injured by getting a box on the ear.

Eyes

A Scout, of course, must have particularly good eyesight; she must be able to see anything very quickly, and to see it a long way off. By practicing your eyes in looking at things at a great distance they will grow stronger. While you are young you should save your eyes as much as possible, or they will not be strong when you get older; therefore avoid reading by lamplight or in the dusk, and also sit with your back or side to the light when doing any work during the day; if you sit facing the light it strains your eyes.

The strain of the eyes is a very common failure with growing girls, although very often they do not know it, and headaches come most frequently from the eyes being strained; frowning on the part of a girl is very generally a sign that her eyes are being strained. Reading in bed brings headaches.

Teeth

Bad teeth are troublesome, and are often the cause of neuralgia, indigestion, abscesses, and sleepless nights.

Good teeth depend greatly on how you look after them when you are young. Attention to the first set of teeth keeps the mouth healthy for the second teeth, which begin to come when a child is seven and these will last you to the end of your life, if you keep them in order.

If one tooth is allowed to decay, it will spread decay in all the others, and this arises from scraps of food remaining between the teeth and decaying there.

A thorough Scout always brushes her teeth inside and outside and between all, just the last thing at night as well as other times, so that no food remains about them to decay. Scouts in camps or in the wilds of the jungle cannot always buy tooth-brushes, but should a tiger or a crocodile have borrowed yours, you can make your teeth just as bright and white as his are by means of a frayed-out-dry, clean stick.

Learn how to make camp tooth-brushes out of sticks. Slippery elm or "dragonroot" sticks for cleaning teeth can be got at chemists' shops as samples.

Measurement of the Girl

It is of paramount importance to teach the young citizen to assume responsibility for her own development and health.

Physical drill is all very well as a disciplinary means of development, but it does not give the girl any responsibility in the matter.

It is therefore deemed preferable to tell each girl, according to her age, what ought to be her height, weight, and various measurements (such as chest, waist, arm, leg, etc.). She is then measured, and learns in which points she fails to come up to the standard. She can then be shown which exercises to practice for herself in order to develop those particular points. Encouragement must afterwards be given by periodical measurements, say every three months or so.

Cards can be obtained from the "Girl Scouts" Office,

which, besides giving the standard measurements for the various ages, give columns to be filled in periodically, showing the girl's remeasurements and progress in development. If each girl has her card it is a great incentive to her to develop herself at odd times when she has a few minutes to spare.

My Physical Development

Date.	Weight.	Height.	Chest Expanded	Neck.	Forearm.	Biceps.

Fill in this page quarterly, the progress shown should be a useful incentive.

Games to Develop Strength

Skipping, rowing, fencing, swimming, tennis, **and** handball are all valuable aids to developing strength.

Use also:—

Staff exercises, to music if possible.   Maze and spiral; follow-my-leader, done at a jog-trot in the open air.   A musical accompaniment when possible.   If done indoors, all the windows in the room must be kept open top and bottom.   Sing the tune.

FLAGS.—Choose sides; each player lays down a flag or a handkerchief at her own goal, and each side tries to capture the flags of the other; once she touches the opponent's flag she cannot be taken prisoner, but goes back with the flag to her side.

Players can rescue a prisoner by touching her in prison. Players should keep moving as much as possible all the time, and try to evade being captured.

PRACTICE throwing at a mark. Put a pebble on the top of a staff and stand at a certain line so many paces off.

Morris dances (old English country dances) and the folk-songs.

ENDURANCE IS USEFUL

Have you not often heard of accidents on the ice?   In the winter of 1895 some schoolgirls were sliding on a frozen canal, when one girl twelve years old ventured into the middle.   Then there was an ominous cracking, and in a moment she was struggling in water many feet deep.

Miss Alice White, a teacher, happened to witness the accident.   Notwithstanding the warnings of several persons standing on the towing-path, who assured her it was most dangerous, she at once went on the ice and approached as close to the hole as she dared with safety. She then lay down at full length, so as to more equally distribute her weight, and tried to seize the struggling child. But under her weight the ice broke, and the brave girl was precipitated into the cold water. The by-standers shouted to her to forsake the child, and at least save her own life, but she did nothing of the kind. She held on to her precious burden, and literally fought her way out. Piece after piece of the ice broke off, but she at length reached the bank in a state of great exhaustion. Her hands were cut in many places by the sharp ice, but they were wounds of which any one might well have been proud. Miss White was only sixteen years old, and it was the second time she had saved a life.

Laying a pole or a branch across the hole is a good plan.

An Easy Way to Grow Strong

It is possible for any girl, even though she may be small and weak, to make herself into a strong and healthy woman if she takes the trouble to do a few body exercises every day. They take only about ten minutes, and do not require any kind of apparatus.

This should be practiced every morning, the first thing on getting up, and every evening before going to bed. A girl of ten years should weigh at least fifty pounds, the average height at that age being forty-nine inches. The value of this exercise is much increased if you think of the object of each move while you are doing it, and if you are very particular to breathe the air in through your nose. A great many people who are pale and ill are made so by living in rooms where the windows are seldom opened and the air is full of poisonous gases or germs. Open your windows, especially at the top, every day to let the foul air out.

Do not exercise immediately *after* eating; let your meal be digested.

Girls who have not done these exercises before should begin them gradually with care, bit by bit, doing more every day. Brush your hair, clean your teeth, wash out your mouth and nose, drink a cup of cold water, and then go on with the following exercises.

It is best to carry these out with as few clothes on as possible, either in the open air or close to an open window. The movements should be executed vigorously.

First Series

EXERCISE I.

Stand erect, hands at side.

Count 1. Bend knees deeply with trunk held vertical.

Count 2. Straighten knees and return to an erect position.

Count 3. Let the body fall directly forward until it reaches an angle of 45 degrees, advancing the left foot a long stride to catch the weight of the body, and bringing the closed hands to shoulders, palms forward, elbows close at side, shoulders drawn back and chest out.

Count 4. Bend at the waist without moving the legs and touch the floor with both hands.

Count 5. Return to the third position.

Count 6. Stand erect.

Repeat ten times, using first one foot, then the other. At the end of one week use this exercise fifteen times. Continue to increase the repetitions by fives each week until you can do thirty.

EXERCISE II.

Take five deep breaths, inhaling and exhaling, filling the lower part of the chest, and at the end of the breath expelling all the air you can.

Second Series

EXERCISE I.

Run in place, that is go through the movements of running without gaining ground, twenty steps, rest a minute and do fifty counts.

EXERCISE II.

Lying on the back, hands at side, raise the body and touch the toes with both hands, ten times.

EXERCISE III.

Count 1. Charge sideways, raising the arms sideways to a vertical position.

Count 2. Bend and twist to the left, touching the floor with both hands on the left side of the foot.

Counts 3 and 4. Make the return movements.

Repeat ten times in each direction.

EXERCISE IV.

Deep breathing eight times.

Third Series

EXERCISE I.

Bend knees deeply, fifteen times.

EXERCISE II.

Lying face downward, hands at side, raise the head and chest from the floor as far as possible.

EXERCISE III.

Lying face downward, head resting on the folded arms, raise each leg upward and backward from the hip with straight knee, ten times.

EXERCISE IV.

Lying on the back, hands under head, raise both legs with straight knees to a vertical position, toes pointed upward, ten times.

EXERCISE V.

Charge obliquely forward left, arms in line with the body and rear leg; touch the floor and return, making it a four-count exercise.

Repeat ten times in each direction.

EXERCISE VI.
Run in place for one minute, rest and repeat.

EXERCISE VII.
Take ten deep breaths.

HOME LIFE

Housewifery

Every Girl Scout is as much a "hussif" as she is a girl. She is sure to have to "keep house" some day, and whatever house she finds herself in, it is certain that that place is the better for her being there.

Too many odds and ends and draperies about a room are only dust-traps, and rugs or carpet squares, which can be taken up easily, are better than nailed down carpets. Keep all the furniture clean and bright. Fresh air, soap, and water are the good housewife's best allies. Bars of soap should be cut up in squares, and kept for six weeks before being used. This hardens it, and makes it last longer.

In scrubbing boarded floors, the secret is not to deluge the floor; change the water in the pail frequently.

In the work of cleaning, think out your plan beforehand, so as not to dirty what has been cleaned. Plan certain times for each kind of work, and have your regular days for doing each thing.

PASTE-BOARDS AND DEAL TABLES.—Scrub hard the way of the grain. Hot water makes boards and tables yellow. Rinse in cold water, and dry well.

SAUCEPANS.—New saucepans must not be used till they have first been filled with cold water and a little soda, and boiled for an hour or so, and must be well scoured. After basins or saucepans have been used fill them at once with cold water to the brim; this will prevent anything hardening on the saucepan, and will make cleaning easier.

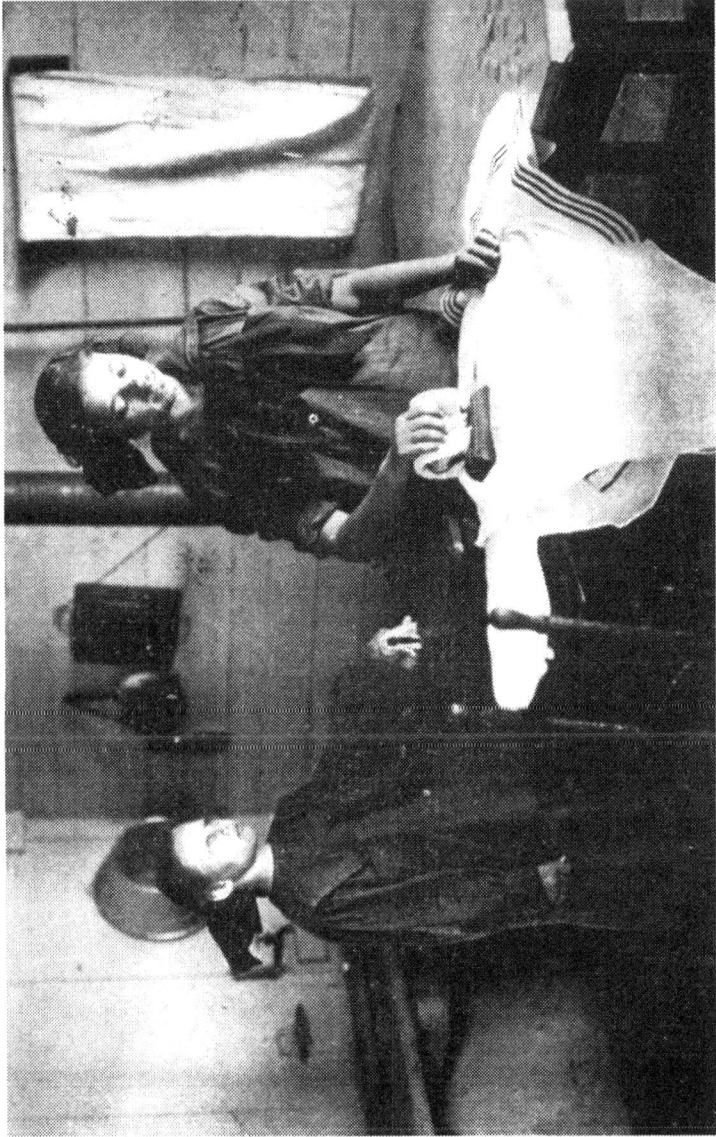

Needlework

"A stitch in time saves nine." We cannot agree with this favorite saying, because it saves so many more than nine, besides saving time and preventing untidiness.

Tailors, who are such neat workers, will say that they never pin their work first. If you are not a tailor, it is much better to place your work, before you begin, with plenty of pins. You will never get straight lines or smooth corners if you do not plan and place it all first, just as it has got to be, and tack it there.

Have you noticed that thread is very fond of tying itself into a bow; but this can be prevented by threading the cotton into the needle before you cut it off the reel, making your knot at the end you cut.

In rough measures, one inch is equivalent to the distance across a twenty-five-cent piece, and a yard is from nose to thumb, as far as you can reach. Needlework is good for all of us; it rests and calms the mind. You can think peacefully over all the worries of Europe whilst you are stitching. Sewing generally solves all the toughest problems, chiefly other peoples'.

Pillow lace needs a little more attention, but is a lovely art which girls can easily master. The writer was taught to make the flowers of Honiton lace by a little Irish girl, and the variations you can invent are endless. You would find a good sale for insertion lace of the Torchon patterns. Make your own pillow, and buy some cheap bobbins to begin learning with, and do not try fine work at first. Learn to spin wool and thread; a spinster can earn money in this way.

The Girl Scouts' Patch

We don't know whether you ever did such a thing as burn a hole in your dress, but we have, and if it is in the front, oh, dear! what will mother say. Now, there is a very good way that Girl Scouts have of making it all right and serviceable; they put in a piece and darn it in all round. If possible, get a piece of the same stuff, then it will not fade a different tint, and will wear the same as the rest. You may undo the hem and cut out a bit, or perhaps you may have some scraps left over from cutting out your dress.

The piece must be cut three or four inches larger than the hole, and frayed out on all four sides. Trim the hole with your scissors neatly all round quite square with the thread. Then lay your piece over the hole— of course on the back or "wrong side"—and tack it there with cotton. Now take a darning needle, and thread each thread in turn, and darn each one into the stuff. If the ends of stuff are very short, it is best to run your needle in and out where you are going to darn, and then, before pulling it through, thread it with the wool. This patching is excellent for table-linen.

We once had an aunt who was a thorough old Scout, and was rather proud of her mending. She always said that she did n't mind what colored cotton you gave her to sew with, because her stitches hardly ever showed, they were so small, and also she put them inside the stuff. If she was putting on a patch to blue stuff, she could do it with red cotton, and you would never have noticed it on the right side; her stitches were all under the edge. Or else she sewed it at the back, on the wrong side, so that it looked perfectly neat.

If you are not able to match the wool for a darn, it is a good plan to use the ravelings of the stuff itself. Sometimes, away in the country, you can't go to a shop and you have nothing like the piece you want to mend. A Scout would turn it inside out and undo a little of the hem, and ravel out the edge. Suppose you were to cut a hole in the front of your blue serge skirt; if you darn it with the ravelings of the turnings of the seam or the hem, that will be exactly the same color and the same

thickness as your dress. No wool you could buy would match as well. Or if you want to mend a jersey or knitted gloves, you never could buy such a good match—the same sized wool and the tints.

Damask table-cloths should be darned to match the pattern, following the flowers of the design, and large holes may be mended like the "Scouts' Patch" just described. To sew on buttons properly, leave them loose enough for the iron to push. On washing articles have your threads long enough to make a little stalk to the button, which is wound round before finishing. Your needle should be sloped out to all sides, so as to take up fresh stuff farther out than the holes in the button.

Scouts may make many useful presents in their spare time, such as cretonne covered blotters or frames, mittens, warm felt slippers (for which woolly soles can be bought), pen-wipers, pin-cushions, and needle-books. They could also make articles for their hospitals, such as night-clothing, soft caps, handkerchiefs, pillow-cases, and dusters.

HOME COOKING

There is a legend in Turkey that when a rich man is engaged to marry a lady he can break it off if she is not able to cook him a dish of dates in a different way every day for a whole month. A friend of ours did somewhat the same in trying a new cook; he always tested them with nothing but cutlets for a fortnight. The real test of a good cook is to see how little food she wastes. She uses up all the scraps, and old bits of bread are baked for making puddings and for frying crumbs; she sees that nothing goes bad, and she also buys cleverly. Those who do not understand cookery waste money.

Perfect cleanliness and neatness should be insisted on, or your food will be bad and unwholesome.

Eggs

Is an egg lighter or heavier when cooked? An experienced cook is experienced in eggs. There are "new laid" eggs which are fresh and "fresh" eggs which are not; there are "cooking" eggs which are liable to squeak. Eggs are safe in their shells, and think you don't know whether they are fresh or not, or whether they are raw. Any egg can be thrown out of a first-floor window on to the lawn without the shell breaking; it falls like a cat, right end upwards, and this is not a boiled egg, either! You can tell that because it will not spin on the table, so it must have been a raw egg. A cooked egg would spin.

To tell a stale egg, you will see it is more transparent at the *thick* end when held up to the light.

Fresh eggs are more transparent in the *middle*. Very bad eggs will *float* in a pan of water.

Poached Eggs

Break each egg separately into a cup. When your water is boiling fast, drop in an egg sharply. Use a large deep pan, with salt and vinegar in the water. Lift the egg very carefully in a ladle before it is set too hard. Place the eggs all round a soup plate, pour over them a nice sauce made with flour and butter, a little milk, and some grated cheese and salt.

STOCK POT.—Keep a pot going all day, into which you can put any broken-up bones or scraps left over, to make nourishing broth. Clean turnips, carrots, and onions improve it. Before using let it get cold, so as to skim off the fat.

HOME HEALTH
Contributed by Dr. Thomas D. Wood.

1. **Dust** (carries germs and bacteria)—
   a. Must be kept out of the house by
      1. Being careful not to bring it in on shoes or clothing.
      2. By really removing the dust when cleaning, not just brushing it from place to place with dry brushes and dust cloths.

   b. Tools needed—
      1. Vacuum cleaner (if possible).
      2. Brooms and brushes of different kinds.
      3. Mops.
      4. Dust cloths of cotton, outing flannel and wool.
      5. Soft paper.

   c. Methods of cleaning—
      1. Cleansing and putting away all small movable articles first.
      2. Wiping walls, pictures, floor, furniture, woodwork, etc., using damp cloths and brushes, if possible, so that no dust can fly, and gathering all dust on a dustpan that has a damp paper on it to collect dust.
      3. Airing and sunning each room while cleaning.
      4. Wiping window shades at least once a week.
      5. Cleaning hangings often and laundering table and cushion covers.
      6. Keeping every corner, drawer, and closet aired, cleansed, sunned and in order at all times to prevent accumulation of dust, germs and household pests.
      7. Keeping all bathroom furnishings spotless and sweet, always drying after cleansing.
      8. Scalding all cleaning tools and drying in sunshine, if possible, before putting away.

2. Care of the Bedroom—

Hygiene of the Bedroom—

1. Substances that tend to make the bedroom unhealthy are—
   a. Excretions from lungs, skin, kidneys.
   b. Street dust that has settled on clothing in day.
2. Relation of personal habits to healthfulness of the bedroom—
   a. Leave outside wraps outside bedroom, if at all possible, at least until they have been well dusted.
   b. Never put into the closet clothing that has been next to the skin during the day. Such articles should be aired by an open window during the night.
   c. A bath each day at some time and a thorough cleansing of face, hands and feet before going to bed will prevent much dust and body excretions from accumulating on bed clothing.
3. Preparation for the Night—
   a. Remove counterpane and fold carefully.
   b. Protect blanket by covering with a sheet or other light covering.
   c. Open windows from top and bottom.
   d. Hang used clothing to air.
4. Care of Room on Rising—
   a. Remove bed clothing and hang by open window in the sun.
   b. Air night clothing before hanging away.
   c. If a washstand is used, empty all bowls and jars, soap dishes, etc., wash and dry them before leaving the room for breakfast.
   d. When thoroughly aired, make the bed and put the room in order.

5. Making the Bed Properly—

   a. Mattress must have been turned. There should be a covering for the mattress under the first sheet.

   b. Put on the under sheet, tucking it securely under mattress at top, bottom and sides.

   c. Put on upper sheet and blankets, tucking in at bottom only.

   d. Turn upper sheet down over blankets.

   e. Cover with counterpane and place on well-beaten pillows.

6. Weekly Cleaning—

   a. Mattress, rugs, and unwashable hangings should be removed to some place in outdoor air and sunshine, beaten and dusted.

   b. Closets must be cleaned and dusted first, then used to store all small articles from room after they have been thoroughly cleaned.

   c. Clean walls, pictures, woodwork, floors, windows and shades.

   d. Put room in order.

   f. Such care of the rooms of a house make regular "housecleaning" spells unnecessary.

3. Kitchen Sanitation—

Do not wash—

   1. Iron (range).
   2. Brass and copper.
   3. Tin.
   4. Zinc.
   5. Aluminum, nickel, silver.

To clean metals of grease, use kerosene, gasoline, benzine, naphtha, chloroform, soap suds.

    b. Care of Sink—
      1. Pour dishwater through a sieve.
      2. Greasy water must be changed into a soap or dissolved before being poured down to drain.
      3. Flush sink drain three times a week with boiling sal soda solution, one pint sal soda to three gallons of water. Use at least two quarts.
    c. Kitchen needs same treatment for general cleanliness, removal of dust, etc., as other rooms and walls. Woodwork — floor should be often washed thoroughly in hot soapsuds, rinsed and dried to be sure no germs develop where food is being prepared.
    d. Care of Ice Chest—
      1. Should be emptied and thoroughly washed and dried at least twice a week to make it a wholesome place for food.

4. Cellar—

    1. Must be kept as free of dust and rubbish as the kitchen.
    2. No decaying vegetables or fruit must be found in it.

5. Door-Yard and Out-Building—

    1. Grass and growing things, especially if sprayed with water daily, will help keep dust out of houses.
    2. Rubbish of any kind should be burned, for it is in such places that flies and mosquitoes breed.
    3. Grass should be kept cut and lawns raked to keep mosquitoes from breeding.
    4. No manure from domestic animals should be allowed to be exposed on the premises, for in such material the typhoid fly lays its eggs.
    5. Barns and out-houses should be screened.

6. To Clean Fruits and Vegetables—

1. Garden soil is the home of a multitude of small forms of life, many quite harmless, but some organisms causing disease. For instance, germs of tetanus are found in dust and soil.
2. Top-dressing or fertilizer used to enrich the soil may contain such disease germs.
3. If fruits or vegetables come from the market instead of the garden they are quite as likely to have dust and bacteria clinging to them.
4. It is necessary, therefore, to wash all vegetables and fruits thoroughly before using.

7. How to Wash Fruit and Vegetables—

1. Put berries and small fruits in a colander, a few at a time, and dip lightly down and up in a basin of water, being careful not to crush the fruit.
2. Wash strawberries with hulls on.
3. Firm fruits, as grapes, cherries, etc., can be washed by standing the colander under the cold water faucet for some time.
4. Lettuce is best washed under the cold water faucet and celery needs scrubbing with a brush.
5. Apples from exposed fruit stands should be soaked for some time and carefully dried.

8. Fresh Foods Are Best—

1. Celery, cabbage, apples, pumpkins, beets, squash, white and sweet potatoes, etc., can be kept fresh for out of season use if carefully cleansed and stored away in a dry, cool, dark place.

9. Methods of Preserving Foods—

1. Salting.
2. Pickling.
3. Refrigeration.
4. Canning.
5. Preserving.
6. Drying or evaporation.

10. **Method of Preserving Eggs—**
   1. Packing in coarse salt.
   2. Cover with water-glass in large stone jars, set in cool place.

11. **Care of Milk—**
   1. Use certified milk or inspected milk.
   2. Wash bottle top before removing cover.
   3. Pour milk in pans that have been scalded and drained dry in the sun or, in damp weather, by the stove.
   4. As soon as cool enough put in refrigerator or in coolest place possible, as milk spoils very quickly unless kept cold.

12. **Care of Meat—**
   1. Wash thoroughly as soon as it arrives.
   2. Place on clean pan of aluminum, porcelain or some such ware.
   3. Place in refrigerator until ready to cook.

13. **General Rules For Care of Food—**
   1. Keep food clean—(personal cleanliness, washing food).
   2. Keep food dry.
   3. Keep food cool.
   4. Care for food left from each meal. If carefully put away it can be used and not wasted.

Inspected Milk—
   1. Comes from sanitary farms where cows, cases and bottles are reasonably clean; the rules are much less strict than for certified milk.
   2. Cannot by law contain more than 500,000 germs in each teaspoonful, while certified milk contains not more than 50,000 germs.

Pasteurized Milk—
   1. Method recommended by Department of Health of Chicago. In a small tin pail place a saucer.

On the saucer stand the bottle of milk (leaving the cap on the bottle). Now put sufficient hot water (not so hot as to break the bottle) into the pail to fill same to within three or four inches of the top of the bottle, and then stand the pail and its contents on the top of the stove. The instant the water begins to boil remove the bottle of milk from the pail and cool it as rapidly as possible. Keep the bottle of milk in the ice box and keep the cap on the bottle when not in use. When you remove the cap do so with a clean prong, and be careful that the milk side of the cap does not come in contact with anything dirty. None but inspected or certified milk should be used.

Milk should be kept covered with clean cheese cloth to prevent dust getting in.

Water—
1. Water will carry germs of typhoid fever, cholera, etc.
2. Boiling and cooling all water that might be suspected.

Unprotected and Exposed Food—
a. Prevention—
   1. Be sure of a pure water supply (inspection of Board of Health).
   2. Cleanse all foods properly before eating.

House Fly—
a. Why it is a Disease Carrier—
   1. Breeds in filth where disease germs are found.
   2. Construction of feet, legs, body, wings, etc., favorable for catching and holding great numbers of filth and disease germs.
b. How to Fight the Fly—
   1. Catch all flies that get in the house.

2. Keep food covered.
3. Trap flies out of doors.
4. Screen all windows of houses, barns or outbuildings.

Mosquito—

1. Carries germs of malaria and yellow fever.
2. Turn over every pail or tub that may hold water.
3. Pick up old tin cans and bottles and put them where rain cannot fill them.
4. Screen rain barrels and cisterns so mosquitoes cannot get to the water and lay eggs.
5. Screen the wash water if it is left standing over night.
6. Change water every day in drinking pans for birds and animals.

Rats—

Prevention—
Get rid of them by trapping and killing.

HINTS TO HOUSEKEEPERS

How to Clean Wire Window Screens

Rub down with Kerosene oil outside and inside.

Three Primary Colors *are, Red, Blue and Yellow.*

Polishing Floors

One quart of turpentine to one quarter ($\frac{1}{4}$) pound of beeswax. Warm, taking care not to let any fire reach the turpentine. Rub in the floor with flannel and polish with hard brush. A little powdered burnt umber mixed in gives a nice brown stain.

To Put Away Flannels

First thoroughly air and beat them, then wrap up with cedar chips, refuse tobacco, or camphor, and wrap in newspapers, being careful to close every outlet to keep out moths.

Babcock Test

The Babcock test is a test for determining the butter fat in milk.

Bottles are devised which are known as Babcock milk bottles, and are registered to show the per cent. of fat in milk. A certain amount of milk is mixed with a certain amount of Commercial Sulphuric acid of a specific gravity 1.83 which is added by degrees and thoroughly shaken up with the milk. Enough distilled water is added to fill the bottle. The mixture is then centrifuged in a Babcock Centrifuge, and the centrifuged fat read in per cent. on the neck of the bottle.

119

The Official Travelers' Babcock Test can be purchased from the Creamery Package Manufactory Co., Chicago Ill., and costs between $5.00 and $6.00.

All utensils used in dairy work should be sterilized by steaming or boiling for five minutes.

How to Cure Hams

Rub one tablespoonful of Saltpetre into the face of each ham; let it remain one day. Literally cover the ham with salt and pack it in a closed box. Leave it in box as many days as there are pounds to the ham.

Take it out, wash in warm water; cover the face of the ham with black pepper, and smoke it ten days with green hickory or red-oak chips.

Care of Children

Mrs. Benson writes: " There is no way in which a girl can help her country better than by fitting herself to undertake the care of children. She should learn all she can about them, and take every opportunity of helping to look after these small Girl Scouts and Boy Scouts of the future."

An infant cannot tell you its wants, but a Scout with a knowledge of the needs of children, what to feed them on, and the rules for good health, may save many a baby, for she never knows how soon the precious gift of some child's life may be placed in her hands.

Baby does not know that fire will burn, or that water will drown one, so you need to guard him. Baby requires the proper food to build up a healthy body. He prefers milk for the first months of his life, and even up till three years old he takes mostly milk; and as a baby cannot digest flour, bread, corn-flour, and such things are so much poison to him. They may injure a little baby's health for life. As has been said to older children,

let him keep quiet after eating. Even up to three years old, Baby's food must be chiefly milk—biscuits, puddings, and fruit being gradually added. He is very particular about his milk being fresh and good. Baby is extremely punctual. He feels it keenly if you do not feed him at the fixed hour, and will very likely let you know it, and woe betide you if he finds out that you have not properly scalded out his bottle before and after each meal.

When his digestion is not right, his appetite will not be so good. Digestion means that the food you eat is turned into muscle and brain and bone.

We eat onions to make bone, and oats to make brain, but Baby must not be allowed such food till he is older. What is *indigestion?* It means not only uncomfortable pains in the middle of the night, but also that you have not used up the food you ate, and that food is going bad inside you, and making bad blood. Eat only the foods that you know you can digest comfortably. Do not give Baby too much at a time, or he will not be able to digest it, and keep him to plain food.

Air

Sun and air are life-giving. Put a pale withering plant or human being into the sun, and each will recover health. Give a baby plenty of fresh air, out of doors if you can, but avoid draughty places. Air the rooms well. You know, too, that the air inside the bed-clothes is impure, so do not let Baby sleep with his head under the sheet; tuck it in under his chin. You remember what air did in curing illness in the case of the expressman's children. He had two boys and three little girls all beginning to have consumption, and constantly requiring a doctor at great expense. He got the happy idea of putting them all into his cart when he started out very early on his work, and he drove them about every morning till school time. Every one of them soon got well, and became strong and healthy.

Bath

No one can be healthy unless she is extremely clean. Baby will want his bath daily, with soap and warmish water. He likes to kick the water and splash, as long as you support his head. Before starting on this swimming expedition, you should have all his clothes, warm, by you, and all that you will want must be within reach, and he expects a warm flannel on your knees to lie on. You must carefully dry all the creases in his fat body for him, with a soft towel.

Illnesses

What will you do when you suddenly find that baby is ill. Call in the doctor? Yes—that is, if there is one. But when there is no doctor! You will at once think of all the First Aid you have learnt, and what you know of nursing.

Drugs are bad things. You may ruin a child by giving it soothing drugs and advertised medicines. They sometimes produce constipation. Never neglect the bowels if they become stopped, or you may bring on inflammation. Children's illnesses often are brought on by damp floors; you can trace them to the evening that the boards were washed. · A flood of water could not dry without damping the room and the children.

Bowed legs come from walking too soon. It does baby good to lie down and kick about, for crawling and climbing exercise his muscles.

The best remedy, if you find a child suffering from convulsions, is to place it in a warm bath, as hot as your bare elbow can endure.

Childhood is the time to form the body; it cannot be altered when you are grown up.

Clothing

Children's clothes should be warm but light, and the feet and legs should be kept warm and dry. To put on their stockings, turn the toe in a little way, and poke the toes into the end, then pull over a little at a time, instead of putting the foot in at the knee of the stocking. Put the left stocking on the right foot next day, so as to change them every day.

Flannelette is made of cotton, so it is not warm like wool, and it catches fire easily, as cotton-wool does.

Rubber is most unhealthful, and causes paralysis. Don't sit on rubber or on oilcloth unless covered, and never put rubber next to the skin.

Thermometers

To convert a given number of degrees Fahrenheit into Centigrade, deduct 32, multiply by 5, and divide by 9. To convert into Réaumur, deduct 32, multiply by 4, and divide by 9. To convert degrees Centigrade into Fahrenheit, multiply by 9, divide by 5, and add 32. To convert Réaumur into Fahrenheit, multiply by 9, divide by 4, and add 32.

The diagram shows corresponding degrees.

Beat of Pulse per minute

Pulse beat for normal person:
Infant before age of one year, 130 to 115 beats per minute.

Infant up to two years of age, 115 to 130 beats per minute.

Adult, 70 to 80 beats per minute. Adult in old age, 70 to 60 in normal health.

Part V

FIRST AID

THE National Red Cross Society award certificates in First Aid to girls over sixteen years old only, but any Girl Scout can win the Girl Scout Ambulance badge by passing an examination on the first three chapters of the Woman's Edition of the Red Cross Abridged Text-Book on First Aid.

This training of the Girl Scouts awakens taste for hospital work. The scope of this book is insufficient for a complete course of instruction in hospital work, so it is best for the leaders to have lectures, lessons, and demonstrations. There is danger in a "little knowledge" of such an important subject. So we shall only say that the one important Scout precept of obeying orders is in a hospital of paramount importance. Disobedience is certainly a *crime*.

Nosebleed

Slight nosebleed does not require treatment; no harm results from it. When severe nosebleed occurs, loosen the collar (do not blow the nose), apply cold to the back of the neck by means of a key or a cloth wrung out in cold water; a roll of paper under the upper lip between it and the gum will help; when bleeding still continues shove a cotton or a gauze plug into the nostrils leaving it there until the bleeding stops.

Eyes

Dust, flies, or cinder in the eye. Get the person's head well back, seize the upper eyelash and pull the upper lid well forward over the lower, press it against the latter as it slips back into place, and if the fly is beneath the upper lid it will be left on the lower lid. If this fails, place a match on the upper eyelid, catch the eyelashes and turn the lid over the match, and if you can see the cause of the trouble remove it with the corner of a handkerchief or use a camel's-hair brush. A drop of castor-oil in the eye soothes it afterwards. For lime in the eye use a weak solution of vinegar and water.

FIRST AID TO INJURED

Fire constitutes a danger, especially if there is a panic where the fire starts. Never throw away a lighted match, it may fall on inflammable material and start fire. Reading in bed is dangerous, as if you go to sleep the bed-clothes may catch fire. If you must dry your clothes by a fire watch them carefully.

Cut away all dry grass around a fire in camp.

Never carry a light into a room that smells strongly of escaped gas; never handle gunpowder with matches in your pocket.

How to Put out Fire

If your clothing catches fire don't run for help, that will fan the flames; lie down, roll up in an overcoat or rug. If nothing can be found to roll about you, roll over slowly beating out the flames with your hands. If another person is on fire throw him on the ground and smother the fire with a rug away from the face.

What to Do in Case of Fire

Show coolness and presence of mind; throw water (a few bucketfuls will often put out the fire), or blankets, woolen clothing, sand, ashes, dirt, or even flour on fire.

If you discover a fire sound the alarm on the street fire-alarm post, or telephone to the Fire Department. The doors of a house or a room that is on fire should be closed to prevent draughts spreading the flames.

While searching a burning house tie a wet handkerchief over the nose and mouth. Remember that within six inches of the floor there is no smoke; when you have difficulty in breathing, crawl along the floor with the head low, dragging any one you have rescued behind you. Tie the insensible person's hands together and put them over your head. You can then crawl along the floor dragging the rescued person with you.

Never jump from the window unless the flames are so close that it is your only means of escape. If outside a burning building put mattresses and bedding piled high to break the jumper's fall and get a strong rug to hold, to catch the jumper, and let many people hold the rug. In country districts organize a bucket brigade; two lines of girls from water to fire—pass buckets, jugs, tumblers, or anything that will hold water from girl to girl and throw water on the fire, passing buckets back by another line of girls.

Rescue from Drowning

There are four practical methods of bringing a drowning person to land.

Fig. 1

1. If quiet, turn him on his back, and grip him by the head so that the palms of the hands cover the ears, and swim on the back. Keep his face above water (Fig. 1).

2. In case of struggling, turn him on his back. Then grip his arms just above the elbows and raise them until they are at right angles to his body, and swim on the back (Fig. 2).

Fig. 2

Fig 3.

3. If the arms are difficult to grasp, push your arms under those of the subject, bend them upwards, and place your hands, with the fingers separated, flat on his chest, the thumbs resting on his shoulder joints. Swim on the back (Fig. 3).

4. In rescuing a swimmer with cramp or exhausted, or a drowning person who is obedient and remains quiet, the person assisted must place his hands on the rescuer's shoulders close to the neck at arm's length, turn on his back, and lie perfectly still with the head well back. Here the rescuer is

Fig. 4

uppermost; and, having his arms and legs free, swims with the breast stroke. This is the easiest method, and enables the rescuer to carry the person a longer distance without much exertion (Fig. 4).

Release

A drowning person will sometimes grip his would-be rescuer in such a manner as to render it impossible to tow him to land. The three following methods are recommended for releasing oneself when clutched by a drowning person.

1.   **When the rescuer is grasped by the wrists: Extend
the arms** straightforward, bring them down until they
are in a line with the hips, and then jerk the wrists against
the thumbs of the subject.   This will break the hold
(Figs. 5 and 6).

Fig. 5   Fig. 6

Fig. 7

2.   When the rescuer is clasped
round the neck: Take a deep breath
and lean well over the drowning
person.   At the same time, place
the left hand in the small of his
back.   Then pinch the nostrils close
between the fingers of the right,
while resting the palm on his chin,
and push away with all possible
force (Fig. 7).

3.   When the rescuer is clasped
round the body: Take a deep breath
and lean well over as before.   Place
the left hand on the subject's right
shoulder and the right palm on his
chin.   At the same time bring the
right knee against the lower part of
his chest.   Then by means of a
strong and sudden push, stretch
your arms and leap straight out, throwing the whole
weight of your body backwards (Fig. 8).

Fig. 8

Artificial Respiration

When a person is brought to land in an apparently drowned condition lose no time in attempting restoration. Delay may prove fatal. Act at once and work with caution, continuous energy, and perseverance. Life has, in many cases, been restored after long hours of unceasing work. In all cases send for a doctor as soon as possible. Meanwhile proceed at once to clear the water out of the patient's lungs. The following method is the simplest and is called the Schäfer system, after the inventor. Incline the patient face downwards and the head downwards, so that the water may run out

Fig. 9

of his mouth, and pull his tongue forward. After running the water out of the patient, place him on his side with his body slightly hanging down, and keep the tongue hanging out. If he is breathing let him rest; if he is not breathing, you must at once endeavor to restore breathing artificially. Here are Professor Schäfer's own instructions:

Fig. 10

1. Lay the patient face downwards with arms extended and the face turned to the side.

2. Don't put a cushion or any support under the chest. Kneel or squat alongside or astride of the patient facing towards his head.

3. Place your hands on the small of the patient's back, one on each side, with thumbs parallel and nearly touching.

4. Bend forward with the arms straight, so as to allow the weight of your body to fall on your wrists, and then make a firm, steady downward pressure on the loins

of the patient, while you count slowly, "one—two—three."

5.   Then swing your body backward so as to relieve the pressure and without removing your hands, while you count slowly, "one—two."

Continue this backward and forward movement, alternately relieving and pressing the patient's stomach against the ground in order to drive the air out of his chest and mouth, and allowing it to suck itself in again, until gradually the patient begins to do it for himself.

Fig. 11

The proper pace for the movement should be about twelve pressures to the minute. As soon as the patient is breathing you can leave off the pressure; but watch him, and if he fails you must start again till he can breathe for himself.

Then let him lie in a natural position and set to work to get him warm by putting hot flannels or bottles of hot water between his thighs, and under the arms and against the soles of his feet. Wet clothing should be taken off and hot blankets rolled round him. The patient should be disturbed as little as possible and encouraged to sleep while carefully watched for at least an hour afterwards.

Ice Rescue

To rescue a person who has broken through the ice, you should first tie a rope around your own body and have the other end tied or held in shore. Then get a long board or a ladder, or the limb of a tree, crawl out on this and push it out so that the person in the water may reach it. If nothing can be found on which to support your weight don't attempt to walk to the person to be rescued, but lie flat on your face and crawl out to him, thus so much less weight bears on the ice at one point than walking. Remember, if you break through the ice yourself, that if you try to crawl on the broken ice it will break again with you; better support yourself on edge of ice and await rescue.

Gas and Sewer Gas

Never go to sleep in a room where the gas is burning low. As gas may escape into the room, very big fires burning in sleeping rooms are dangerous, especially in charcoal stoves. In underground sewers and wells dangerous gases are found; if a lighted candle will not burn in such a place it is certain the air will be dangerous for any one entering it.

In rescuing a person from a place filled with gas, take a few deep breaths before entering, carry him quickly out without breathing yourself. Gas will not be found near the floor of a building, so you may be able to crawl out where it would be dangerous to walk.

Treating and Bandaging the Injured

A fracture is the same thing as a broken bone. When the bone pierces through the skin it is called a compound fracture. When it does *not*, a simple fracture.

If you have to deal with a broken leg or arm, and can't get a doctor at once, make the patient lie down.

Place the leg in the same position as sound one, and hold it in splints made of anything that is stiff and rigid like a *flat* board (that is better than a round pole) or a limb broken from a tree. Shingles make excellent splints.

In applying splints, they should extend beyond the next joint above and the next joint below the broken point.   Otherwise the movement of the joint will cause the broken part to move.

With a broken thigh, the splint should be very long, extending from armpit to below the feet; a short splint just below the knee will do for the inner splint.

Splints may be tied on with handkerchiefs; tie firmly, but not so tight as to cause severe pain.

In a fractured thigh it is well to bind the broken leg to the sound one by two or three pieces of cloth around both.

The clothing around the leg makes a padding for the splints unless it is thin summer clothing, in which case straw and leaves should be put between the splint and the leg, or arm.

Fractures of the leg and arm are treated the same way, with splints on inner and outer sides of broken bone.

A sling will be required with fractures of the arm; this may be made with triangular bandage or triangular neck handkerchief or piece torn from your skirt or petticoat. Red Cross outfits are very convenient for injuries.

Compound Fracture

If the sharp edges of the broken bone pierce through the skin, which often happens if splints are not well applied and the person moves, the broken bone again pierces the skin.   If a wound is made by the broken bone, then the wound must be treated first.

Dressing Wounds

All wounds, unless protected from germs, are liable to become infected by matter or pus.   Blood-poisoning or even death may result.   To prevent infection of wound, a sterilized dressing should be applied; this is a surgical dressing which has been treated so that it is free from germs and can be got at any druggist's or can be had in First Aid outfits.   Don't handle a wound with your hands, because even though your hands appear perfectly clean, they are not so; neither is water free from germs, so a wound should never be washed.

If you have no surgical dressing, boil a folded towel fifteen minutes; don't touch the inner surface. Apply inner surface of the towel or a clean unused handkerchief to the wound.

How to Stop Bleeding

Keep a person quiet after severe bleeding from a wound as the bleeding may recommence, and give no stimulants unless patient is very weak.

There are two kinds of blood—that which flows from arteries and the blood which flows from veins; the latter is of a dark color and flows in a steady stream and goes back to the heart. A pad firmly tied on such a wound usually stops the bleeding.

Don't be afraid of leaving a wound exposed to air

When wounds bleed use Red Cross outfit as directed on slip contained in outfit.

If an artery is cut a person may bleed to death in a few minutes. Girls should know that the blood from a cut artery is bright red and flows in spirts and jets.

There are arteries in the throat. The artery in the upper arm is about in a line with the inner seam of the sleeve of your coat.

The artery in the leg runs down from the center line from the point of the hip in the middle of the crotch in a line with the inseam of trousers.

Pressure should be applied by putting your fingers three inches above the crotch and holding it pressed against the bone. You can feel the artery beating under your fingers, but don't put your finger in the wound as it may infect the latter. While you hold the artery some one else should make a tourniquet easily improvised.

9

How to Make a Tourniquet

Tie a handkerchief loosely around the limb and place a cork or a smooth stone, just above your fingers on the artery. When this is placed, put a stick about a foot long under the handkerchief at the outer side of the limb and twist the stick so that the handkerchief gets tight enough to keep the stone or cork pressing on the artery just as your fingers did at first. Tie the stick in position so it will not slip.

Remember that cutting off the circulation for too long is dangerous; don't leave the tourniquet more than an hour. Loosen it and be ready to tighten it quickly if the bleeding recommences.

Another method to stay bleeding from an artery when the injury is below the knee or elbow is to place a pad in the bend and tie the arm or leg bent with the pad tight in the angle of the joint.

If an artery is cut at the throat, hold tightly together the wound to stop the bleeding or the person may die instantly from loss of blood.

The best stimulant in cases where the patient is very weak is aromatic spirits of ammonia. One teaspoonful in a half-glass of water.

Ivy Poisoning

Avoid poison oak or ivy. If poisoned use carbolized vaseline or baking-soda and water made into a thick paste. Apply alcohol first.

To Ease Itching of Midge-Bites

For midge and sand-fly bites use listerine and Eucalyptus—equal quantities—liquid carbonic soap—apply one drop on bite—or preparation sold by druggist.

Frost-Bite

To prevent frost-bite, rub the body when exposed to cc with too little clothing on, because rubbing brings blood the surface. When the part that was cold suddenly has feeling, then to restore warmth rub it first with snow or cc water, then gradually with warm water; if hot water is appli at first it may cause mortification in the frozen part.

Runaway Horses

Don't try to check a runaway horse by standing in fre and waving your arms. The horse only dodges you and ru faster.

Electric Shock

Artificial Respiration should always be promptly given cases of electric shock.

The rescuer must not touch the body of a person touchi a live wire or a third rail unless his own body is thorough insulated.

He must act quickly. He should, if possible, insulate hi self by covering his hands with a rubber coat, rubber sheeti or even several thicknesses of dry cloth. Silk is a good nc conductor. In addition he should complete his insulation standing on a dry board, or a thick piece of dry paper or a dry coat.

Rubber gloves or boots are safer, but they cannot usually immediately available.

If a live wire is under a patient and the ground is dry it w be perfectly safe to stand upon it and pull him off with t bare hands. But they should touch only his clothing and tl must not be wet.

A live wire on a patient may with safety be flipped off wi a dry board or stick. A live wire may be safely cut by an a or hatchet with a dry wooden handle and the electric curre may be short circuited by dropping a crowbar or a poker the wire. They should be dropped on the side from which t current is coming and not on the further side as the latter w not short circuit the current before it has passed through t patient's body. Drop the metal bar, do not place it on t wire or you will then be made a part of the short circuit a receive the current of electricity through your body.

From American Red Cross Text Book on Elementa Hygiene and Home Care of the Sick.

Part VI

PATRIOTISM

History of the Flag

On July 4, 1776, the Declaration of Independence was signed. By this the united colonies dissolved all the ties that bound them to England and became an independent nation, the United States. It was immediately necessary to adopt a new flag, as the new nation would not use the union jack. Congress appointed a committee, consisting of George Washington, Robert Morris, and Colonel Ross, to design a flag. They got Mrs. Betsey Ross, who kept an upholstery shop at 239 Arch Street, Philadelphia, to help plan and to make the new flag. They kept the thirteen stripes of the colonies' flag, and replaced the union jack by a blue field bearing thirteen stars, arranged in a circle. On June 14, 1777, Congress passed the resolution adopting this flag.

Resolved: That the flag of the thirteen United States be thirteen stripes, alternate red and white: that the Union be thirteen stars, white on a blue field, representing a new constellation.

George Washington said: "We take the star from Heaven, the red from our mother country, separating it by white stripes, thus showing that we have separated from her, and the white stripes shall go down to posterity representing liberty."

This new flag was first carried into battle at Fort Stanwix, in August, 1777.

At first when new States came into the Union, a new stripe and a new star were added to the flag, but it was soon evident that the added stripes would make it very unwieldy. So on April 4, 1818, Congress passed this act, to establish the flag of the United States.

SEC. 1. Be it enacted, etc. That from and after the fourth day of July next, the flag of the United States be thirteen horizontal stripes, alternate red and white; that the Union have twenty stars, white in a blue field.

SEC. 2. Be it further enacted, that, on the admission of every new State into the Union, one star be added to the Union of the flag; and that such addition shall take effect on the fourth day of July succeeding such admission.

In our flag today the thirteen stripes symbolize the thirteen original States, and the blue field bears forty-eight stars, one for each State in the Union. The five-pointed star is used, it is said, at Betsey Ross's suggestion. This five-pointed star is the seal of King Solomon, and the sign of infinity. Even the colors of the flag mean something: red stands for valor, blue for justice, and white for purity. The whole flag stands for freedom, liberty, and justice.

Respect Due the Flag

1. The flag should not be hoisted before sunrise nor allowed to remain up after sunset.

2. At retreat, sunset, civilian spectators should stand at attention and give the military salute.

3. When the national colors are passing on parade or review the spectators should, if walking, halt, and if sitting, rise and stand at attention and uncover.

4. When the flag is flown at half-mast as a sign of mourning it should be hoisted to full staff, at the conclusion of the funeral. In placing the flag at half-mast, it should first be hoisted to the top of the staff and then be lowered to position. Preliminary to lowering from half-mast it should first be raised to top.

5. On Memorial Day, May 30th, the flag should fly

at half-mast from sunrise till noon, and at full mast from noon to sunset.

The flag at half-mast is a sign of mourning.
The flag flown upside down is a signal of distress.

America

The first home of social and religious freedom in America was in the Colony of Maryland. When all the other colonies were persecuting every one that did not believe in their own peculiar religious doctrine and making the most invidious social distinctions, Maryland—the Ever Faithful—was a haven of refuge for all. Situated in a middle place among the colonies, her doctrines gradually spread till today the proud boast of America is that she is the home of the free. Had the sentiments of Massachusetts prevailed, we would have had today a most bigoted form of religious government. Had John Locke's Carolina laws lasted, we would have been under a grinding oligarchy. Georgia under Oglethorpe's wise management joined hands with Calvert in Maryland, and the result of their joint efforts for the betterment of mankind is the grand Republic of the United States of today. Adams and Washington, Franklin and Lincoln are names which shine out from the pages of history today, and back of each was a good and honored mother. These were patriots—not politicians or place hunters. Throughout our history the emergency seems always to have found the man. And they have been prepared by our great women. For even if a man has not a wife it is seldom that any great thing is done that is not helped on by a woman. Girls, know your places. They are no mean positions that you are destined to hold. The pages of the history of the future may hold your names in a high and honored place. Do well your part today. The work of today is the history of tomorrow, and we are its makers. So let us strive to show just as grand names on the pages yet unwritten as are inscribed on those that we have for our proud inheritance.

It is not necessary that every Scout should be proficient in all things suggested for practice. All should be able to drill and know the signs—secret and open—for the use of the organization. They should practice the precepts laid down for their guidance and be above all things "the little friend to all" that makes such a distinctive feature in the work and training of every day's meeting of Scouts. Consider it a paramount duty to attend all meetings and get the most out of the opportunities offered you in the American Band of Girl Scouts. Make your duties amusements and your amusements duties. So will you find that you daily increase in usefulness and your pleasure in life will grow broader. In union there is strength. The Union of Scouts is to be a strong union for the good of our nation in the future and an ever-increasing bond for success to ourselves and aid to others.

The Star-Spangled Banner

O say, can you see, by the dawn's early light,
　　What so proudly we hail'd at the twilight's last gleaming?
Whose broad stripes and bright stars, thro' the perilous fight,
　　O'er the ramparts we watched were so gallantly streaming;
And the rocket's red glare, the bombs bursting in air,
Gave proof thro' the night that our flag was still there!
O say, does that star-spangled banner yet wave
O'er the land of the free and the home of the brave?

On the shore, dimly seen thro' the mists of the deep,
　　Where the foe's haughty host in dread silence reposes,
What is that which the breeze, o'er the towering steep,
　　As it fitfully blows, half conceals, half discloses?
Now it catches the gleam of the morning's first beam,
In full glory reflected, now shines on the stream—
'T is the star-spangled banner. O long may it wave
O'er the land of the free and the home of the brave!

And where is that band who so vauntingly swore,
  'Mid the havoc of war and the battle's confusion,
A home and a country they 'd leave us no more?
  Their blood has washed out their foul footsteps' pollution.
No refuge could save the hireling and slave
From the terror of flight, or the gloom of the grave—
And the star-spangled banner in triumph shall wave,
O'er the land of the free and the home of the brave.

O thus be it ever when freemen shall stand
  Between their loved homes and foul war's desolation,
Blest with vict'ry and peace, may the heav'n-rescued land
  Praise the Power that hath made and preserved us a nation.
Then conquer we must, when our cause it is just,
And this be our motto, "In God is our trust"—
And the star-spangled banner in triumph shall wave,
While the land of the free is the home of the brave.

FRANCIS SCOTT KEY.

America

My country, 't is of thee,
Sweet land of liberty,
  Of thee I sing;
Land where my fathers died,
Land of the Pilgrims' pride,
From every mountain side
  Let freedom ring.

My native country, thee,
Land of the noble free,
  Thy name I love;
I love thy rocks and rills,
Thy woods and templed hills;
My heart with rapture thrills
  Like that above.

Let music swell the breeze,
And ring from all the trees
  Sweet freedom's song;
Let mortal tongues awake,
Let all that breathe partake,
Let rocks their silence break,
  The sound prolong!

Our father's God, to Thee,
Author of liberty,
   To Thee we sing:
Long may our land be bright
With freedom's holy light;
Protect us by Thy might,
   Great God, our King.

SAMUEL F. SMITH, 1832.

Allegiance to the Flag

I pledge allegiance to the flag, and to the republic for which it stands; one nation indivisible, with liberty and justice for all.

Girl Scout Salute to the Flag

A salute to the Flag should be the first number on the program of every meeting. Use the Scout full salute. The salute may be accompanied by the words of the pledge. Let the hand reach the forehead on the word **"allegiance,"** pointing, palm outward, to the flag and recite the remaining words with hand still pointing to flag.

READING LIST

BOOKS ON MERIT BADGE SUBJECTS

AMBULANCE:
Emergencies. Gulick, C. E.
Firebrands. Martin, F. E.
Home Nursing. Harrison, E.
Sure Pop and the Safety Scouts. Bailey, R. R.

ASTRONOMY:
Story of the Heavens. Ball, Roberts.
Heavens with an Opera Glass. Serviss, Garrett.
The Friendly Stars. Martin, M. E.
Ways of the Planets. Martin, M. E.
Easy Guide to the Constellations. Gall, James.
Sun Lore of All Ages. Olcott, W. T.

ART:
Composition. Dow.
How to Judge a Picture. Van Dyke.

ARTS AND CRAFTS:
Art Crafting in Metals for Amateurs. Chandler.
Art Crafts for Beginners. Sanford, F. E.
Dan Beard's Books.

BIRDS: (*see also* NATURALIST.)
Birds of Village and Field. Merriam, Florence A.
Birds and Bees. Burroughs, John.
Squirrels and Other Fur Bearers. Burroughs, John.
Sharp Eyes. Gibson, Wm. H.
Chapman's Books on Birds—According to Locality.
Bird Guide. Reed, Chester A.
Bird Craft. Wright, M. A.
How to Attract the Birds. Trafton, G.

BOATSWAIN:
Boys' Outdoor Vacation Book. Verrill, A. H.
Harper's Boating Book for Boys. Verrill, A. H

CHILD NURSE:
Baby Clothing. Hitching, W.
Care and Feeding of Children. Holt, L. E.
Care and Training of Children. Kerr, L.
Care of Milk and Its Use in the Home. U. S. Dept. of Agriculture.

CLERK:
Goodwin's Improved Bookkeeping and Business Manual. Goodwin, J. H.
Handbook of Style. (*Punctuation.*) Houghton, Mifflin.
Modern Business Arithmetic. Curtis, U.
New Practical Typewriting.

COOK, INVALID COOKING:
Boston Cooking-School Cook Book. Farmer, F. A.
Food for the Invalid and the Convalescent. Gibbs, W. S.
Mary Frances Cook Book. Fryer, J. E.
When Mother Lets Us Cook. Johnson, C.

DAIRY MAID:
Dairy Chemistry. Snyder, H.
Milk and Its Products. Wing, H. H.
Official Travelers' Babcock Test. Creamery Package Manufacturing Co., Chicago.

ELECTRICIAN:
A. B. C. of Electricity. Meadowcroft, W. H.
Boy Electrician. Morgan, A. P.
Electricity for Young People. Jenks, T.
Harper's Beginning Electricity. Shafer, D. C.
Harper's Electricity Book for Boys. Adams, J. H.

FARMER:
Bees. (*Farmers' Bulletin 447.*) U. S. Dept. of Agr.
How to Keep Bees. Comstock, A. B.
Hints to Poultry Raisers. (*Farmers' Bulletin 528.*) U. S. Dept. of Agr.
Incubation and Incubators. (*Farmers' Bulletin 236.*) U. S. Dept. of Agr.
Pig Management. (*Farmers' Bulletin 205.*) U. S. Dept. of Agr.
Poultry Management. (*Farmers' Bulletin 287.*) U. S. Dept. of Agr.
First Book of Birds. Miller.
Second Book of Birds. Miller.
Our Home Pets. Miller.
The Garden Book for Young People. Lounsberry.
Bird Stories from Burroughs.
Butterflies and Bees. Morley.
Insect Stories. Kellog.
The Scout Garden. Bennet, F. H.

GARDENS:
Children's Gardens for Pleasure, Health and Education.
    Parsons, H. G.
Garden Primer. Tabor, G.
Harper's Book for Young Gardeners. Verrill, A. H.
School Garden Book. Weed, Clarence.
When Mother Lets Us Garden. Duncan, F.
First Book of Birds. Miller, O. T.
Second Book of Birds. Miller, O. T.
Our Home Pets. Miller, O. T.
Little Gardens for Boys and Girls. Higgins, M.
The Garden Book for Young People. Lounsberry.
Bird Stories. Burroughs.
Butterflies and Bees. Morley.
Insect Stories. Kellog.
The Scout Garden. Bennet, F. H.

HEALTH:
Body at Work. Jewett, F. G.
Good Health. Jewett, F. G.
Personal Hygiene. Pyle.
Handbook Girls' Branch of Public School Athletic League. Burchenal.
The Human Mechanism. Hough & Sedgwick.

HOUSEKEEPER:
Good Housekeeping Magazine. Gilman, E. H.
Housekeeping. (Children's Library of Work and Play.) Gilman, E. H.
How to Live on a Small Income. Hewitt, E. C.
Manual of Household Work and Management. Butterworth.
Mary Frances, Housekeeper. Fryer, J. E.

LAUNDRESS:
Laundry Manual. Balderston, L. R.
Housekeeping. (Children's Library of Work and Play.) Gilman, E. H.

MUSICAL:
Dictionary of Music and Musicians. Gove, G.
Operas that Every Child Should Know. Bacon, M. S.
Stories from the Operas. Davidson.
Story of Music and Musicians. Millie, L. C.
Young People's Story of Music. Whitcomb, I. P.
Intervals, Theory, Chords, and Ear Training. Brown, J. P.

NATURALIST:
Bird-Life. Chapman, F. M.
Bird Neighbors. Blanchan, N.
Flower Guide. Reed, C. A.
Handbook of Birds of Eastern North America. Chapman, F. M.
How to Attract the Birds. Blanchan, N.
How to Know the Wild Flowers. Parsons, F. T.
Land Birds. Reed, C. A.
Nature Library. Doubleday.
Standard Library of Natural History. University Society.
Wild Flowers Every Child Should Know. Stack, F. W.
The American Flower Garden. Blanchen, Neltye.
How to Know the Wild Flowers. Mrs. W. M. S. Dana.
How to Know the Ferns. Parsons, Frances T.
Primer of Forestry. Pinchot, Gifford.
Our Native-Trees. Keeler, Harriet L.

Ways of Wood Fowls. Long, Wm. D.
Secrets of the Woods. Long, Wm. D.
Lives of the Hunted. Seton-Thompson, Ernest.
Wild Animals I Have Known. Seton-Thompson, Ernest.
Jungle Books. Kipling, Rudyard.
Our National Parks. Muir, John.
Earth and Its Story. Hulprin, Angelo.

Naturalist. Trafton.

NEEDLEWOMAN:
Easy Steps in Sewing. Fryer, J. E.
Home Art Crochet Book. Klickmann, F.
Magic of Dress. Gould.
Needlecraft. (*Children's Library of Work and Play.*) Archer, E. A.
Sewing for Little Girls. Foster, O. H.
Three Hundred Things a Bright Girl Can Do. Kelley, L. E.
When Mother Lets Us Sew. Johnson, C.

PIONEER:
Boy's Camp Book. Cave, E.
Boy Scout's Hike Book. Cave, E.
Camp Cookery. Kephart, H.
On the Trail. Beard, L.

SIGNALLING:
Official Handbook for Girls.

SWIMMER:
Swimming. Brewster.

TELEGRAPHIST:
Official Handbook for Boys. Boy Scouts of America.

GENERAL READING

FAMOUS WOMEN:
When I Was a Girl in Italy. Ambrosi, M.
Promised Land. Antin, M.
Lives of Girls Who Became Famous. Bolton, S. K.
Joan of Arc. de Monvel, B.
Girls' Book of Famous Queens. Farmer, L. H.
Life of Mary Lyon. Gilchrist, B. B.
Autobiography of a Tomboy. Gilder, J. L.
Historic Girlhoods. Holland, R. S.
Group of Famous Women. Horton, E.
Story of My Life. Keller, H.
New England Girlhood. Larcom, L.
Heroines that Every Child Should Know. Mabie, H. W.
Louise, Queen of Prussia. Merz, H.
Louisa May Alcott. Moses, B.
Life of Alice Freeman Palmer. Palmer, G. H.
Florence Nightingale. Richards, L. E.
When I Was Your Age. Richards, L. E.
Wonder Workers. Wade, M. H.
Jeanne D'Arc. Wilmot-Buxton.
Queens of England. Strickland.

FAIRY TALES AND FOLK LORE:
Arabian Nights.
Fairy Tales. Andersen, H. C.
Granny's Wonderful Chair. Browne, F.
Alice's Adventures in Wonderland. Carroll, L.
Fairy Tales. Grimm Bros.
Uncle Remus, His Songs and Sayings. Harris.
Celtic Fairy Tales. Jacobs, J.
Blue Fairy Book. Lang, A.
Pinocchio. Lorenzini, C.
Children's Book. Scudder, H. E.

HISTORY OF LITERATURE:
History of the English Language. Lounsbury, T. P.
English Literature for Boys and Girls. Marshall, H. E.
Introduction to American Literature. Pancoast, H. S.

POETRY:
Songs of Innocence. Blake, Wm.
Golden Staircase. Chisholm, L.
Poems of Childhood. Field, E.
Lyra Heroica. Henley, W.
Boy's Percy. Lanier, S.
Nonsense Books. Lear, E.
Story Telling Poems. Olcott, F. J.
Golden Treasury. Palgrave, F. T.
Book of Famous Verse. Repplier, A.
Child's Garden of Verse. Stevenson, R. L.
Golden Numbers. Wiggin, K. D.
Pinafore Palace. Wiggin, K. D.
Posy Ring. Wiggin, K. D.
Lays of Ancient Rome. Macaulay.
Longfellow's Poems. Longfellow.
Lady of the Lake. Scott.
Idylls of the King. Tennyson.
Robin Hood Ballads. Parker.
Rosemary and Rue. Gordon.

STORIES:
Lisbeth Longfrock. Aanrud, A.
Little Men. Alcott, L. M.
Little Women. Alcott, L. M.
Under the Lilacs. Alcott, L. M.
Marjorie Daw. Aldrich, T. B.
Pride and Prejudice. Austen, J.
Little Minister. Barrie, J. M.
Lorna Doone. Blackmore, R. D.
Jane Eyre. Brontë, C. M.
Last Days of Pompeii. Lytton, Bulwer.
Girlhood of Shakespeare's Heroines. Clarke, M. C.
Friend of Cæsar. Davis, W. S.
Egyptian Princess. Ebers, G. M.
Silas Marner. Eliot, G.
Ramona. Jackson, H. H.
Hypatia. Kingsley, C.
Mr. Achilles. Lee, J.
Scottish Chiefs. Porter, J.
Cloister and the Hearth. Reade, C.
Daisy Chain. Yonge, C. M.
Peter and Wendy. Barrie, J. M.
Four Gordons. Brown, E. A.
Peep-in-the-World. Crichton, F.
Hans Brinker. Dodge, M. M.

Lass of the Silver Sword. Dubois, M. C.
Mary's Meadow. Ewing, J. H.
Peterkin Papers. Hale, L. P.
York and a Lancaster Rose. Keary.
Bimbi. Ramée.
Queen Hildegarde. Richards, L. E.
Castle Blair. Shaw, F. E.
Heidi. Spyri, J.
Mother Carey's Chickens. Wiggin, K. D.
David Copperfield. Dickens.
A Tale of Two Cities. Dickens.
The Talisman. Sir Walter Scott.
Little Lord Fauntleroy. Burnett.
Sarah Crewe. Burnett.
Six Girls. Irving, F. B.
John Halifax, Gentleman. Craik, D. M.
Last of the Mohicans. Cooper.
Pathfinder. Cooper.
Deerslayer. Cooper.
Otto of Silver Hand. Pyle.
Merry Adventures of Rab. **Brown.**
Treasure Island. Stevenson.
Black Arrow. Stevenson.
Jackanapes. Ewing.
Nelly's Silver Mine. Jackson.
Robinson Crusoe. De Foe.
Rab and His Friends. Brown.
Bob, Son of Battle. Ollivant.
The Call of the Wild. London.
Master Skylark. Bennett.
The Prince and the Pauper. Twain.
Harold, the Last of the Saxon Kings. Bulwer-Lytton.
The White Company. Doyle, Conan.
Wonderful Adventures of Nils. Lagerlöf.
Tales of Laughter. Smith.
Richard Carvel. Churchill.
Hugh Wynne. Mitchell.
Quentin Durward. Scott.
Ben Hur. Wallace.
Holiday House. Sinclair.
Alice in Wonderland. Carroll.
Just So Stories. Kipling.
Eight Cousins. Alcott.
Juan and Juanita. Baylor.
Black Beauty. Sewell.
Birds' Christmas Carol. Wiggin.
Story of Siegfried. Baldwin.

Swiss Family Robinson. Wyss.
Six to Sixteen. Ewing.
Man Without a Country. Hale.
Tom Brown's School Days. Hughes.
Anne of Green Gables. Montgomery.
Barnaby Lee. Bennett.
Judith Shakespeare. Black.
Colonel's Opera Cloak. Brush.
Smith College Stories. Daskam.
Captains Courageous. Kipling.
Kidnapped. Stevenson.
Rudder Grange. Stockton.
A Gentleman of France. Weyman.
New Chronicles of Rebecca. Wiggin.
Polly Oliver's Problem. Wiggin.
Dove in the Eagle's Nest. Yonge.
Elizabeth and her German Garden. (Anonymous.)
Princess Pricelta's Fortnight. Arnim, M. A.
Days of Bruce. Aguilar.
Tales of King Arthur. Lang.

BOOKS OF REFERENCE FOR MERIT BADGE

BIRDS:

Birds as Weed Destroyers. Pp. 221 to 232. Illus. (From *Year-book,* 1898.) Paper, 5c. *A 1.10: 133.*

Birds that Eat Scale Insects. Pp. 189 to 198. Illus. (From *Yearbook,* 1906.) Paper, 5c. *A 1.10: 416.*

Bookkeeping. Farm Bookkeeping. 1912. 37 pp. Illus. (*Farmers' Bulletin 511.*) Paper, 5c. *A 1.9: 511.*

Does it Pay the Farmer to Protect Birds? Pp. 165 to 178. Illus. (From *Yearbook,* 1907.) Paper, 5c. *A 1.10: 443.*

Economic Value of Predaceous Birds and Mammals. Pp. 187 to 194. Illus. (From *Yearbook,* 1908.) Paper, 5c. *A 1.10: 474.*

Fifty Common Birds of Farm and Orchard. 1913. 31 pp. Illus. (*Farmers' Bulletin 513.*) Paper, 15c. *A 1.9: 513.*

Food of Some Well-Known Birds of Forest, Farm, and Garden. 1912. 35 pp. Illus. (*Farmers' Bulletin 506.*) Paper, 5c. *A 1.9: 506.*

How Birds Affect the Orchard. Pp. 291 to 304. Illus. (From *Yearbook,* 1900.) Paper, 5c. *A 1.10: 197.*

Importation of Game Birds and Eggs for Propagation. 1904. 28 pp. 1 illus. (*Farmers' Bulletin 197.*) Paper, 5c. *A 1.9: 197.*

Importation of Game Birds and Eggs for Propagation. **1904.** 28 pp. 1 illus. (*Farmers' Bulletin 197.*) Paper, 5c. *A 1.9: 197.*

Migratory Movements of Birds in Relation to Weather. Pp. 379 **to** 390. 1 illus. (From *Yearbook*, 1910.) Paper, 5c. *A 1.10: 545.*

Relation of Birds to Fruit Growing in California. Pp. 241 to **254.** (From *Yearbook*, 1904.) Paper, 5c. *A 1.10: 344.*

Some Common Birds in their Relation to Agriculture. Revised, 1904. 48 pp. Illus. (*Farmers' Bulletin 54.*) Paper, 5c. *A 1.9: 54.*

Some Common Game, Aquatic, and Rapacious Birds in Relation **to** Man. 1912. 30 pp. Illus. (*Farmers' Bulletin 497.*) Paper, 5c. *A 1.9: 497.*

HEALTH:

Health and Cleanliness—O'Shea and Kellogg—pp. 54-124.

HOUSEKEEPING:

Butter.

Butter-Making on the Farm. 1905. 31 pp. (*Farmers' Bulletin 241.*) Paper, 5c. *A 1.9: 241.*

Canning Vegetables in the Home. 1909. 16 pp. Illus. (*Farmers' Bulletin 359.*) Paper, 5c. *A 1.9: 359.*

School Lessons on Corn. 1910. 29 pp. Illus. (*Farmers' Bulletin 409.*) Paper, 5c. *A 1.9: 409.*

The Home and Family—Kinne and Cooley—pp. 96-137.

Handbook of Domestic Science and Household Arts—Wilson —pp. 273-276 and 55-58.

FARM HOUSES:

Modern Conveniences for the Farm Home. **1906.** 48 pp. Illus. (*Farmers' Bulletin 270.*) Paper, 5c. *A 1.9: 270.*

FARMERS' BULLETINS:

34. Meats, Composition and Cooking. Paper, 5c.
131. Household Tests for the Detection of Oleomargarine **and** Renovated Butter. Paper, 5c.
154. Home Fruit Garden, Preparation and Care. Paper, 5c.
166. Cheese-Making on the Farm. Paper, 5c.
180. Game Laws for 1903. Paper, 5c.
185. Beautifying the Home Grounds. Paper, 5c.
188. Weeds Used in Medicine. Paper, 5c.
195. Annual Flowering Plants. Paper, 5c.
197. Importation of Game Girds and Eggs for Propagation. **Paper,** 5c.
218. School Garden. 2d revised edition. Paper, 5c.
234. Guinea Fowl and its Use as Food. Paper, 5c.
351. Tuberculin Test of Cattle for Tuberculosis. Paper, 5c.
375. Care of Food in Home, corrected to Mar. 25, 1910. Paper, **5c.**
409. School Lessons on Corn. Paper, 5c.
459. House Flies. Paper, 5c.

468. Forestry in Nature Study. Paper, 5c.
478. How to Prevent Typhoid Fever. Paper, 5c.
506. Food of Some Well-Known Birds of Forest, Farm, and Garden. Paper, 5c.
511. Farm Bookkeeping. Paper, 5c.
513. Fifty Common Birds of Farm and Orchard. Paper, 15c.
525. Raising Guinea Pigs. Paper, 5c.

FARMS:

Figs. Smyrna Fig Culture in United States. Pp. 79 to 106. Illus. (From *Yearbook*, 1900.) Paper, 5c. *A 1.10: 106.*

FOREST FIRES:

Attitude of Lumbermen toward Forest Fires. Pp. 133 to 140. Illus. (From *Yearbook*, 1904.) Paper, 5c. *A 1.10: 337.*
Forestry in Nature Study (with Key to Common Kinds of Trees). 1911. 43 pp. Illus. (*Farmers' Bulletin 468.*) Paper, 5c. *A 1.9: 468.*
Grosbeaks. Our Grosbeaks and their Value to Agriculture. 1911. 14 pp. Illus. (*Farmers' Bulletin 456.*) Paper, 5c. *A 1.9: 456.*
Headache Mixtures. Harmfulness of Headache Mixtures (containing Acetanilid, Antipyrin, and Phenacetin). 1909. 16 pp. (*Farmers' Bulletin 377.*) Paper, 5c. *A 1.9: 377.*

PERFUMERY:

Can Perfumery Farming Succeed in United States? Pp. 377 to 3 Illus. (From *Yearbook*, 1898.) Paper, 5c. *A 1.10: 135.*

PLANTS:

Plants Useful to Attract Birds and Protect Fruit. Pp. 185 to 196. (From *Yearbook*, 1909.) Paper, 5c. *A 1.10: 504.*
School Exercises in Plant Production. 1910. 48 pp. Illus. (*Farmers' Bulletin 408.*) Paper, 5c. *A 1.9: 408.*

POISONOUS PLANTS:

Some Poisonous Plants of Northern Stock Ranges. Pp. 305 to 324. Illus. (From *Yearbook*, 1900.) Paper, 5c. *A 1.10: 206.*

School Garden. 2d revised edition, 1909. 41 pp. Illus. (*Farmers' Bulletin 218.*) Paper, 5c.

Yearbook. (Separates.)

414. Cage-Bird Traffic of United States. Paper, 10c.
485. Manufacture of Flavoring Extracts. Paper, 5c.

Farmers' Bulletins

(These Bulletins can be obtained in Washington Agricultural Department for five cents.)

Woman's Edition of Red Cross Abridged Text-Book on First Aid, can be obtained for 35 cents from Girl Scout Headquarters, 527 Fifth Avenue, New York City.

Elementary Hygiene and Home Care of Sick, by Jane Delano.

INDEX

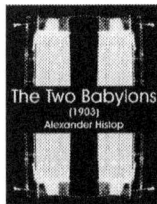

The Two Babylons
Alexander Hislop

QTY

You may be surprised to learn that many traditions of Roman Catholicism in fact don't come from Christ's teachings but from an ancient Babylonian "Mystery" religion that was centered on Nimrod, his wife Semiramis, and a child Tammuz. This book shows how this ancient religion transformed itself as it incorporated Christ into its teachings....

Religion/History — Pages:358

ISBN: *1-59462-010-5* MSRP *$22.95*

The Power Of Concentration
Theron Q. Dumont

It is of the utmost value to learn how to concentrate. To make the greatest success of anything you must be able to concentrate your entire thought upon the idea you are working on. The person that is able to concentrate utilizes all constructive thoughts and shuts out all destructive ones...

Self Help/Inspirational — Pages:196

ISBN: *1-59462-141-1* MSRP *$14.95*

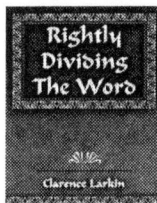

Rightly Dividing The Word
Clarence Larkin

The "Fundamental Doctrines" of the Christian Faith are clearly outlined in numerous books on Theology, but they are not available to the average reader and were mainly written for students. The Author has made it the work of his ministry to preach the "Fundamental Doctrines." To this end he has aimed to express them in the simplest and clearest manner..

Religion — Pages:352

ISBN: *1-59462-334-1* MSRP *$23.45*

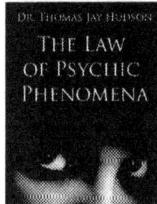

The Law of Psychic Phenomena
Thomson Jay Hudson

"I do not expect this book to stand upon its literary merits; for if it is unsound in principle, felicity of diction cannot save it, and if sound, homeliness of expression cannot destroy it. My primary object in offering it to the public is to assist in bringing Psychology within the domain of the exact sciences. That this has never been accomplished..."

New Age — Pages:420

ISBN: *1-59462-124-1* MSRP *$29.95*

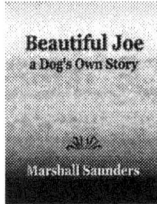

Beautiful Joe
Marshall Saunders

When Marshall visited the Moore family in 1892, she discovered Joe, a dog they had nursed back to health from his previous abusive home to live a happy life. So moved was she, that she wrote this classic masterpiece which won accolades and was recognized as a heartwarming symbol for humane animal treatment...

Fiction — Pages:256

ISBN: *1-59462-261-2* MSRP *$18.45*

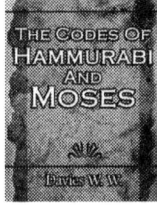

The Codes Of Hammurabi And Moses - W. W. Davies

The discovery of the Hammurabi Code is one of the greatest achievements of archaeology, and is of paramount interest, not only to the student of the Bible, but also to all those interested in ancient history...

Religion — Pages:132

ISBN: *1-59462-338-4* MSRP *$12.95*

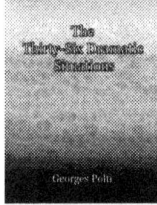

The Thirty-Six Dramatic Situations
Georges Polti

An incredibly useful guide for aspiring authors and playwrights. This volume categorizes every dramatic situation which could occur in a story and describes them in a list of 36 situations. A great aid to help inspire or formalize the creative writing process...

Self Help/Reference — Pages:204

ISBN: *1-59462-134-9* MSRP *$15.95*

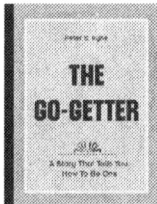

The Go-Getter
Kyne B. Peter

QTY

The Go Getter is the story of William Peck.He was a war veteran and amputee who will not be refused what he wants. Peck not only fights to find employment but continually proves himself more than competent at the many difficult test that are throw his way in the course of his early days with the Ricks Lumber Company...

Business/Self Help/Inspirational — Pages:68

ISBN: *1-59462-186-1* MSRP *$8.95*

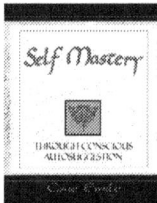

Self Mastery
Emile Coue

Emile Coue came up with novel way to improve the lives of people. He was a pharmacist by trade and often saw ailing people. This lead him to develop autosuggestion, a form of self-hypnosis. At the time his theories weren't popular but over the years evidence is mounting that he was indeed right all along...

New Age/Self Help — Pages:98

ISBN: *1-59462-189-6* MSRP *$7.95*

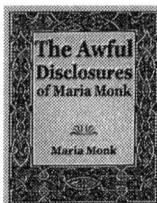

The Awful Disclosures Of Maria Monk

"I cannot banish the scenes and characters of this book from my memory. To me it can never appear like an amusing fable, or lose its interest and importance. The story is one which is continually before me, and must return fresh to my mind with painful emotions as long as I live..."

Religion — Pages:232

ISBN: *1-59462-160-8* MSRP *$17.95*

As a Man Thinketh
James Allen

"This little volume (the result of meditation and experience) is not intended as an exhaustive treatise on the much-written-upon subject of the power of thought. It is suggestive rather than explanatory, its object being to stimulate men and women to the discovery and perception of the truth that by virtue of the thoughts which they choose and encourage..."

Inspirational/Self Help — Pages:80

ISBN: *1-59462-231-0* MSRP *$9.45*

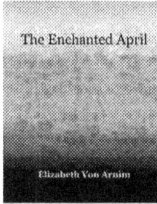

The Enchanted April
Elizabeth Von Arnim

It began in a woman's club in London on a February afternoon, an uncomfortable club, and a miserable afternoon when Mrs. Wilkins, who had come down from Hampstead to shop and had lunched at her club, took up The Times from the table in the smoking-room...

Fiction — Pages:368

ISBN: *1-59462-150-0* MSRP *$23.45*

Holland - The History Of Netherlands
Thomas Colley Grattan

Thomas Grattan was a prestigious writer from Dublin who served as British Consul to the US. Among his works is an authoritative look at the history of Holland. A colorful and interesting look at history....

History/Politics — Pages:408

ISBN: *1-59462-137-3* MSRP *$26.95*

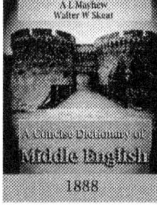

A Concise Dictionary of Middle English
A. L. Mayhew
Walter W. Skeat

The present work is intended to meet, in some measure, the requirements of those who wish to make some study of Middle-English, and who find a difficulty in obtaining such assistance as will enable them to find out the meanings and etymologies of the words most essential to their purpose...

Reference/History — Pages:332

ISBN: *1-59462-119-5* MSRP *$29.95*

www.bookjungle.com *email: sales@bookjungle.com fax: 630-214-0564 mail: Book Jungle PO Box 2226 Champaign, IL 61825*

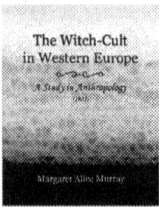

The Witch-Cult in Western Europe
Margaret Murray

QTY

The mass of existing material on this subject is so great that I have not attempted to make a survey of the whole of European "Witchcraft" but have confined myself to an intensive study of the cult in Great Britain. In order, however, to obtain a clearer understanding of the ritual and beliefs I have had recourse to French and Flemish sources...

Occult   Pages:308
ISBN: *1-59462-126-8*   MSRP *$22.45*

The Science Of Psychic Healing
Yogi Ramacharaka

This book is not a book of theories it deals with facts. Its author regards the best of theories as but working hypotheses to be used only until better ones present themselves. The "fact" is the principal thing the essential thing to uncover which the tool, theory, is used...

New Age/Health   Pages:180
ISBN: *1-59462-140-3*   MSRP *$13.95*

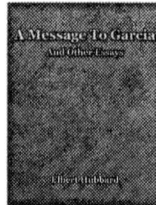

Bible Myths
Thomas Doane

In pursuing the study of the Bible Myths, facts pertaining thereto, in a condensed form, seemed to be greatly needed, and nowhere to be found. Widely scattered through hundreds of ancient and modern volumes, most of the contents of this book may indeed be found; but any previous attempt to trace exclusively the myths and legends...

Religion/History   Pages:644
ISBN: *1-59462-163-2*   MSRP *$38.95*

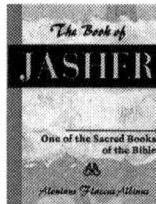

Tertium Organum
P. D. Ouspensky

A truly mind expanding writing that combines science with mysticism with unprecedented elegance. He presents the world we live in as a multi dimensional world and time as a motion through this world. But this isn't a cold and purely analytical explanation but a masterful presentation filled with similes and analogies...

New Age   Pages:356
ISBN: *1-59462-205-1*   MSRP *$23.95*

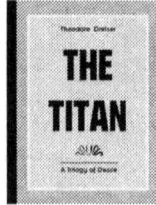

Advance Course in Yogi Philosophy
Yogi Ramacharaka

"The twelve lessons forming this volume were originally issued in the shape of monthly lessons, known as "The Advanced Course in Yogi Philosophy and Oriental Occultism" during a period of twelve months beginning with October, 1904, and ending September, 1905."

Philosophy/Inspirational/Self Help   Pages:340
ISBN: *1-59462-229-9*   MSRP *$22.95*

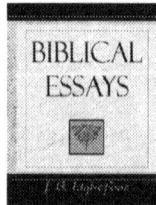

Ambassador Morgenthau's Story
Henry Morgenthau

"By this time the American people have probably become convinced that the Germans deliberately planned the conquest of the world. Yet they hesitate to convict on circumstantial evidence and for this reason all eye witnesses to this, the greatest crime in modern history, should volunteer their testimony..."

History   Pages:472
ISBN: *1-59462-244-2*   MSRP *$29.95*

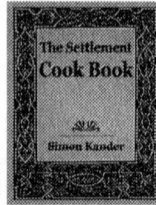

The Aquarian Gospel of Jesus the Christ
Levi Dowling

A retelling of Jesus' story which tells us what happened during the twenty year gap left by the Bible's New Testament. It tells of his travels to the far-east where he studied with the masters and fought against the rigid caste system. This book has enjoyed a resurgence in modern America and provides spiritual insight with charm. Its influences can be seen throughout the Age of Aquarius.

Religion   Pages:264
ISBN: *1-59462-321-X*   MSRP *$18.95*

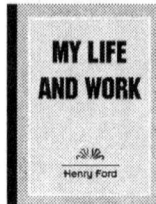

Philosophy Of Natural Therapeutics
Henry Lindlahr

QTY

We invite the earnest cooperation in this great work of all those who have awakened to the necessity for more rational living and for radical reform in healing methods...

Health/Philosophy/Self Help   Pages:552
ISBN: *1-59462-132-2*   MSRP *$34.95*

A Message to Garcia
Elbert Hubbard

This literary trifle, A Message to Garcia, was written one evening after supper, in a single hour. It was on the Twenty-second of February, Eighteen Hundred Ninety-nine, Washington's Birthday, and we were just going to press with the March Philistine...

New Age/Fiction   Pages:92
ISBN: *1-59462-144-6*   MSRP *$9.95*

The Book of Jasher
Alcuinus Flaccus Albinus

The Book of Jasher is an historical religious volume that many consider as a missing holy book from the Old Testament. Particularly studied by the Church of Later Day Saints and historians, it covers the history of the world from creation until the period of Judges in Israel. It's authenticity is bolstered due to a reference to the Book of Jasher in the Bible in Joshua 10:13

Religion/History   Pages:276
ISBN: *1-59462-197-7*   MSRP *$18.95*

The Titan
Theodore Dreiser

"When Frank Algernon Cowperwood emerged from the Eastern District Penitentiary, in Philadelphia he realized that the old life he had lived in that city since boyhood was ended. His youth was gone, and with it had been lost the great business prospects of his earlier manhood. He must begin again..."

Fiction   Pages:564
ISBN: *1-59462-220-5*   MSRP *$33.95*

Biblical Essays
J. B. Lightfoot

About one-third of the present volume has already seen the light. The opening essay "On the Internal Evidence for the Authenticity and Genuineness of St John's Gospel" was published in the "Expositor" in the early months of 1890, and has been reprinted since...

Religion/History   Pages:480
ISBN: *1-59462-238-8*   MSRP *$30.95*

The Settlement Cook Book
Simon Kander

A legacy from the civil war, this book is a classic "American charity cookbook," which was used for fundraisers starting in Milwaukee. While it has transformed over the years, this printing provides great recipes from American history. Over two million copies have been sold. This volume contains a rich collection of recipes from noted chefs and hostesses of the turn of the century...

How-to   Pages:472
ISBN: *1-59462-256-6*   MSRP *$29.95*

My Life and Work
Henry Ford

Henry Ford revolutionized the world with his implementation of mass production for the Model T automobile. Gain valuable business insight into his life and work with his own auto-biography... "We have only started on our development of our country we have not as yet, with all our talk of wonderful progress, done more than scratch the surface. The progress has been wonderful enough but..."

Biographies/History/Business   Pages:300
ISBN: *1-59462-198-5*   MSRP *$21.95*

www.bookjungle.com *email: sales@bookjungle.com fax: 630-214-0564 mail: Book Jungle PO Box 2226 Champaign, IL 61825*

QTY

The Rosicrucian Cosmo-Conception Mystic Christianity by *Max Heindel*	ISBN: *1-59462-188-8* **$38.95**

The Rosicrucian Cosmo-conception is not dogmatic, neither does it appeal to any other authority than the reason of the student. It is: not controversial, but is: sent forth in the, hope that it may help to clear.. New Age Religion Pages 646

Abandonment To Divine Providence by *Jean-Pierre de Caussade* ISBN: *1-59462-228-0* **$25.95**

"The Rev. Jean Pierre de Caussade was one of the most remarkable spiritual writers of the Society of Jesus in France in the 18th Century. His death took place at Toulouse in 1751. His works have gone through many editions and have been republished... Inspirational/Religion Pages 400

Mental Chemistry by *Charles Haanel* ISBN: *1-59462-192-6* **$23.95**

Mental Chemistry allows the change of material conditions by combining and appropriately utilizing the power of the mind. Much like applied chemistry creates something new and unique out of careful combinations of chemicals the mastery of mental chemistry... New Age Pages 354

The Letters of Robert Browning and Elizabeth Barret Barrett 1845-1846 vol II ISBN: *1-59462-193-4* **$35.95**
by *Robert Browning* and *Elizabeth Barrett* Biographies Pages 596

Gleanings In Genesis (volume I) by *Arthur W. Pink* ISBN: *1-59462-130-6* **$27.45**

Appropriately has Genesis been termed "the seed plot of the Bible" for in it we have, in germ form, almost all of the great doctrines which are afterwards fully developed in the books of Scripture which follow... Religion Inspirational Pages 420

The Master Key by *L. W. de Laurence* ISBN: *1-59462-001-6* **$30.95**

In no branch of human knowledge has there been a more lively increase of the spirit of research during the past few years than in the study of Psychology, Concentration and Mental Discipline. The requests for authentic lessons in Thought Control, Mental Discipline and... New Age/Business Pages 422

The Lesser Key Of Solomon Goetia by *L. W. de Laurence* ISBN: *1-59462-092-X* **$9.95**

This translation of the first book of the "Lernegton" which is now for the first time made accessible to students of Talismanic Magic was done, after careful collation and edition, from numerous Ancient Manuscripts in Hebrew, Latin, and French... New Age Occult Pages 92

Rubaiyat Of Omar Khayyam by *Edward Fitzgerald* ISBN: *1-59462-332-5* **$13.95**

Edward Fitzgerald, whom the world has already learned, in spite of his own efforts to remain within the shadow of anonymity, to look upon as one of the rarest poets of the century, was born at Bredfield, in Suffolk, on the 31st of March, 1809. He was the third son of John Purcell... Music Pages 172

Ancient Law by *Henry Maine* ISBN: *1-59462-128-4* **$29.95**

The chief object of the following pages is to indicate some of the earliest ideas of mankind, as they are reflected in Ancient Law, and to point out the relation of those ideas to modern thought. Religion History Pages 452

Far-Away Stories by *William J. Locke* ISBN: *1-59462-129-2* **$19.45**

"Good wine needs no bush, but a collection of mixed vintages does. And this book is just such a collection. Some of the stories I do not want to remain buried for ever in the museum files of dead magazine-numbers an author's not unpardonable vanity..." Fiction Pages 272

Life of David Crockett by *David Crockett* ISBN: *1-59462-250-7* **$27.45**

"Colonel David Crockett was one of the most remarkable men of the times in which he lived. Born in humble life, but gifted with a strong will, an indomitable courage, and unremitting perseverance... Biographies New Age Pages 424

Lip-Reading by *Edward Nitchie* ISBN: *1-59462-206-X* **$25.95**

Edward B. Nitchie, founder of the New York School for the Hard of Hearing, now the Nitchie School of Lip-Reading, Inc, wrote "LIP-READING Principles and Practice". The development and perfecting of this meritorious work on lip-reading was an undertaking... How-to Pages 400

A Handbook of Suggestive Therapeutics, Applied Hypnotism, Psychic Science ISBN: *1-59462-214-0* **$24.95**
by *Henry Munro* Health/New Age Health Self-help Pages 376

A Doll's House: and Two Other Plays by *Henrik Ibsen* ISBN: *1-59462-112-8* **$19.95**

Henrik Ibsen created this classic when in revolutionary 1848 Rome. Introducing some striking concepts in playwriting for the realist genre, this play has been studied the world over. Fiction/Classics/Plays 308

The Light of Asia by *sir Edwin Arnold* ISBN: *1-59462-204-3* **$13.95**

In this poetic masterpiece, Edwin Arnold describes the life and teachings of Buddha. The man who was to become known as Buddha to the world was born as Prince Gautama of India but he rejected the worldly riches and abandoned the reigns of power when... Religion/History/Biographies Pages 170

The Complete Works of Guy de Maupassant by *Guy de Maupassant* ISBN: *1-59462-157-8* **$16.95**

"For days and days, nights and nights, I had dreamed of that first kiss which was to consecrate our engagement, and I knew not on what spot I should put my lips..." Fiction/Classics Pages 240

The Art of Cross-Examination by *Francis L. Wellman* ISBN: *1-59462-309-0* **$26.95**

Written by a renowned trial lawyer, Wellman imparts his experience and uses case studies to explain how to use psychology to extract desired information through questioning. How-to/Science Reference Pages 408

Answered or Unanswered? by *Louisa Vaughan* ISBN: *1-59462-248-5* **$10.95**

Miracles of Faith in China Religion Pages 112

The Edinburgh Lectures on Mental Science (1909) by *Thomas* ISBN: *1-59462-008-3* **$11.95**

This book contains the substance of a course of lectures recently given by the writer in the Queen Street Hall, Edinburgh. Its purpose is to indicate the Natural Principles governing the relation between Mental Action and Material Conditions... New Age/Psychology Pages 148

Ayesha by *H. Rider Haggard* ISBN: *1-59462-301-5* **$24.95**

Verily and indeed it is the unexpected that happens. Probably if there was one person upon the earth from whom the Editor of this, and of a certain previous history, did not expect to hear again... Classics Pages 380

Ayala's Angel by *Anthony Trollope* ISBN: *1-59462-352-X* **$29.95**

The two girls were both pretty, but Lucy who was twenty-one who supposed to be simple and comparatively unattractive, whereas Ayala was credited, as her Bombwhat romantic name might show, with poetic charm and a taste for romance. Ayala when her father died was nineteen... Fiction Pages 484

The American Commonwealth by *James Bryce* ISBN: *1-59462-286-8* **$34.45**

An interpretation of American democratic political theory. It examines political mechanics and society from the perspective of Scotsman James Bryce Politics Pages 572

Stories of the Pilgrims by *Margaret P. Pumphrey* ISBN: *1-59462-116-0* **$17.95**

This book explores pilgrims religious oppression in England as well as their escape to Holland and eventual crossing to America on the Mayflower, and their early days in New England... History Pages 268

www.bookjungle.com *email: sales@bookjungle.com fax: 630-214-0564 mail: Book Jungle PO Box 2226 Champaign, IL 61825*

QTY

The Fasting Cure *by Sinclair Upton*   ISBN: *1-59462-222-1*   **$13.95**
In the Cosmopolitan Magazine for May, 1910, and in the Contemporary Review (London) for April, 1910, I published an article dealing with my experiences in fasting. I have written a great many magazine articles, but never one which attracted so much attention...   New Age/Self Help/Health Pages 164

Hebrew Astrology *by Sepharial*   ISBN: *1-59462-308-2*   **$13.45**
In these days of advanced thinking it is a matter of common observation that we have left many of the old landmarks behind and that we are now pressing forward to greater heights and to a wider horizon than that which represented the mind-content of our progenitors...   Astrology Pages 144

Thought Vibration or The Law of Attraction in the Thought World   ISBN: *1-59462-127-6*   **$12.95**
by William Walker Atkinson   *Psychology/Religion Pages 144*

Optimism *by Helen Keller*   ISBN: *1-59462-108-X*   **$15.95**
Helen Keller was blind, deaf, and mute since 19 months old, yet famously learned how to overcome these handicaps, communicate with the world, and spread her lectures promoting optimism. An inspiring read for everyone...   Biographies/Inspirational Pages 84

Sara Crewe *by Frances Burnett*   ISBN: *1-59462-360-0*   **$9.45**
In the first place, Miss Minchin lived in London. Her home was a large, dull, tall one, in a large, dull square, where all the houses were alike, and all the sparrows were alike, and where all the door-knockers made the same heavy sound...   Childrens/Classic Pages 88

The Autobiography of Benjamin Franklin *by Benjamin Franklin*   ISBN: *1-59462-135-7*   **$24.95**
The Autobiography of Benjamin Franklin has probably been more extensively read than any other American historical work, and no other book of its kind has had such ups and downs of fortune. Franklin lived for many years in England, where he was agent...   Biographies/History Pages 332

Name	
Email	
Telephone	
Address	
City, State ZIP	

☐ Credit Card   ☐ Check / Money Order

Credit Card Number	
Expiration Date	
Signature	

Please Mail to: Book Jungle
PO Box 2226
Champaign, IL 61825
or Fax to: 630-214-0564

ORDERING INFORMATION

web: *www.bookjungle.com*
email: *sales@bookjungle.com*
fax: *630-214-0564*
mail: *Book Jungle PO Box 2226 Champaign, IL 61825*
or PayPal *to sales@bookjungle.com*

Please contact us for bulk discounts

DIRECT-ORDER TERMS

20% Discount if You Order Two or More Books
Free Domestic Shipping!
Accepted: Master Card, Visa, Discover, American Express